NELSON MANDELA

and Apartheid
in World History

Titles *in World History*

NELSON MANDELA
and Apartheid
in World History

Ann Graham Gaines

Enslow Publishers, Inc.
40 Industrial Road   PO Box 38
Box 398   Aldershot
Berkeley Heights, NJ 07922 Hants GU12 6BP
USA   UK

http://www.enslow.com

Library of Congress Cataloging-in-Publication Data

Gaines, Ann Graham.
    Nelson Mandela and apartheid in world history / Ann Graham Gaines.
       p. cm. — (In world history)
    Includes bibliographical references and index.
    ISBN 0-7660-1463-0
    1. Mandela, Nelson, 1918– —Juvenile literature. 2. Presidents—
South Africa—Biography—Juvenile literature. 3. Political prisoners—
South Africa—Biography—Juvenile literature. 4. Apartheid—Juvenile
literature. 5. South Africa—Race relations—Juvenile literature. 6. South
Africa—Politics and government—20th century—Juvenile literature. [1.
Mandela, Nelson, 1918– . 2. Presidents—South Africa. 3. Apartheid—
South Africa. 4. Blacks—South Africa—Biography. 5. Nobel prizes—
Biography.]   I. Title. II. Series.
DT1974.G35   2001
968.06'5'092—dc21

                                         00-010369

Printed in the United States of America

10 9 8 7 6 5 4 3 2 1

To Our Readers: All Internet Addresses in this book were active and appropriate
at the time we went to press. Any comments or suggestions can be sent by e-mail
to Comments@enslow.com or to the address on the back cover.

Illustration Credits: Archive Photos, pp. 9, 112; Courtesy of the South
African Consulate General, New York, p. 94; Enslow Publishers, Inc.,
pp. 6, 16, 32, 38, 52, 96; Library of Congress, pp. 15, 23, 26, 28, 31, 35, 42,
56, 92; © The Nobel Foundation, pp. 90, 98; United Nations, p. 70; UN
Photo 186835/C. Sattleberger, p. 50; UN Photo 177913/H. Vassal, p. 65.

Cover Illustration: Courtesy of the South African Consulate General,
New York (Inset); © Digital Vision Ltd. (Background).

Contents

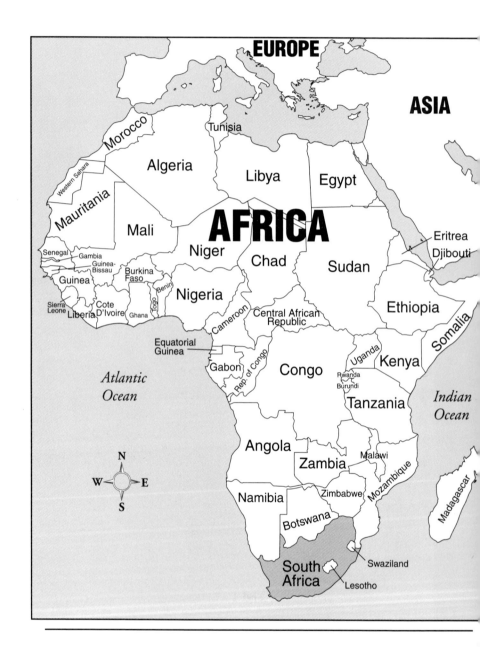

South Africa (shaded) has had a long and turbulent history.

Chapter 1

The Nobel Peace Prize

On December 10, 1993, South Africans Nelson Mandela and F. W. de Klerk made headlines in newspapers around the world. Together, they accepted the prestigious Nobel Peace Prize.

The men stood side by side showing off their medals after ceremonies in Oslo, Sweden. They differed greatly in appearance and background. Mandela was a stately, six-foot four-inch, gray-haired, seventy-five-year-old black man. De Klerk was a fifty-seven-year-old, balding, rotund, white man. Both had been born to influential families. De Klerk's great-grandfather, grandfather, and father had all been important in South African politics. Mandela's father had been a tribal chief. However, the two men had hardly grown up in the same way.

De Klerk was an Afrikaner—a white South African with Dutch ancestors who spoke the Afrikaans language. He had enjoyed a life of privilege, never wanting for food or shelter. He had plenty of money to buy luxuries. He had had a tremendously successful political career, and was elected president of South Africa in 1989.

Mandela, on the other hand, had endured a hard life. He had suffered hunger and other discomforts. Like all black South Africans of his age, Mandela been a victim of apartheid, the racial policy the government of South Africa used for over forty years to segregate (separate by race) its society. Apartheid had forced blacks and other nonwhites to live in separate communities and obey separate laws. For twenty-seven years, Mandela had been held in prison, serving time for having fought against apartheid. But even there, he had continued to fight for the rights of his people. By the time he was released, he had become a symbolic figure, an inspiration both to black South Africans fighting for their rights and to other human rights activists around the globe.

In its announcement concerning the prize, the Nobel Peace Prize committee said that both Mandela and de Klerk had "personal integrity and great political courage."[1] It awarded them the peace prize because, after a difficult struggle, they had finally brought about radical political change in South Africa.

The South African government, which had held Mandela in prison since 1962, had expressed interest in

F. W. de Klerk (left) and Nelson Mandela (right) worked together to make dramatic changes in South Africa.

releasing Mandela from prison in 1985. Other countries put pressure on South Africa to do so. But Mandela refused to leave prison unless certain conditions were met. Although he wanted freedom, he knew his imprisonment was a powerful political symbol. He wanted apartheid ended and the political organizations that had been banned to be allowed to meet once again. The president before de Klerk, Pieter Botha, had never been willing to meet Mandela's demands. But de Klerk was.

The year after his election as president, de Klerk had ordered Mandela released from prison. Then Mandela and de Klerk began to work together to end apartheid. The Nobel committee said it had awarded the prize in recognition of achievements Mandela and de Klerk had made thus far. It wanted the award to be seen "as a pledge of support for the forces of good, in the hope that the advance towards equality and democracy will reach its goal in the very near future."[2]

When the prize was announced, Mandela and de Klerk were actually engaged in a political battle. Together they had succeeded in bringing about the first election in decades in which black South Africans would be able to vote along with whites. Now the two men were running against each other, each seeking to become president of South Africa.

Each man expressed great joy when the announcement was made that jointly they would receive the Nobel prize. De Klerk was relieved that he had brought his government through a difficult period.

Mandela took an even longer view. Interested in the history of his people from the time he was a child, he saw himself as part of a fight that had been going on for five hundred years. He considered himself the representative of millions of people who had dared to fight for their rights. He knew it was the protests of many black and other nonwhite South Africans that was bringing apartheid to an end.

In the speech Mandela delivered when he received the Nobel prize, he spoke of his hope that the black children of South Africa would soon no longer suffer from hunger or disease, and that they could finally receive a decent education. Their parents would no longer fear being arrested, imprisoned, tortured, or killed for fighting for their rights.

Mandela later summed up his own life, writing,

I have walked [a] long road to freedom. I have tried not to falter; I have made missteps along the way. But I have discovered the secret that after climbing a great hill, one only finds that there are many more hills to climb. I have taken a moment here to rest, to steal a view of the glorious vista that surrounds me, to look back on the distance I have come.

Mandela enjoyed his freedom. But he knew there was much more for him to do. He wanted to help South Africa create a new society. And so he said, "But I can rest only for a moment, for with freedom comes responsibilities, and I dare not linger, for my long walk is not yet ended."[3]

Chapter 2

South Africa

To understand how much suffering apartheid caused and how hard it was to end, one must know something about South Africa. This nation covers the southern-most section of the continent of Africa. It is bordered by the Atlantic Ocean to the west and the Indian Ocean to the east. It is mountainous near its shores. Inland lies plateau.

South Africa is large, both in terms of its size and its population. In 1990, South Africa had a population of approximately 40 million. Of those, 35 million were black and 5 million were white. Despite the much larger number of blacks, for many years, the white minority held all political power.

South Africa is also distinguished by its wealth. It exports more gold than any other nation on Earth.

Ancient South Africa

For tens of thousands of years, the native peoples of South Africa were hunter-gatherers. About two thousand years ago, people known as the Khoikhoi, or Hottentots, began to raise livestock. Societies evolved that valued livestock very highly. Leaders were those who owned the most sheep and cattle.

A thousand years ago, people in southern Africa belonged to many different clans. They spoke a variety of languages. Even today, black South Africans consider themselves part of clans, rather than a single race.[1]

From its beginning, the history of South Africa has been characterized by conflict. Some of these conflicts have gone on for generations. Most have been over land. Some especially valuable resources, such as water, have also caused many fights among the people of South Africa.

Europeans Arrive

What would become the nation of South Africa was visited first by the Portuguese. Toward the end of the fifteenth century, Portugal was searching for an eastward route to the East Indies. They wanted to go there to buy spices to sell back home for high prices. In 1488, Bartholomew Diaz commanded ships that sailed south around the Cape of Good Hope, the southern tip of the continent of Africa. It was only after Diaz turned back north that his sailors sighted land. After they

13

landed, the natives of southern Africa saw Europeans for the first time.

In 1495, explorer Vasco da Gama finally succeeded in sailing around Africa to the Indies. His first encounter with natives in South Africa was friendly. They traded with each other. Although a misunderstanding arose in which the Khoikhoi wounded three or four of da Gama's Portuguese with spears, da Gama and his company would land in southern Africa three more times.

The Portuguese dominated the spice trade for about a century. Their ships continued to land in southern Africa, but the Portuguese showed no interest in building a colony there. The area could not give them the spices and ivory they were looking for. They did not realize then that there was a great deal of gold in Africa.

In 1595, a Dutchman named Cornelius Houtman sailed around the Cape of Good Hope. By this time, sailors from many European nations were making the voyage around the southern tip of Africa. But it was the Dutch who eventually took control of the spice trade from the Portuguese.

In the early seventeenth century, both Dutch and British trading companies sent ships to the East Indies. One big problem faced the captains of their ships. The voyage took so long that their crews ran out of fresh water, fruits and vegetables (without which sailors could contract scurvy), and other supplies. They needed a place to stock up on supplies during

Vasco da Gama was one of the first European explorers to reach South Africa.

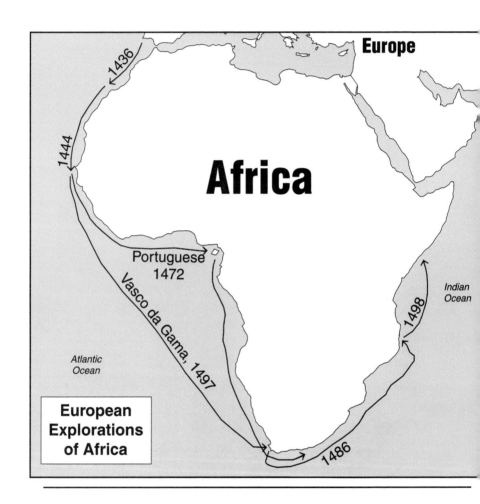

European explorers sailed around Africa and soon began setting up
colonies that would drastically change the lives of the native people.

the voyage. Looking back, South Africa seemed to be a logical place for them to have made a regular stop.

In 1619, representatives of the Dutch East India Company and the British East India Company met to discuss their mutual need for a calling station along the way to the Indies, where ships could rest their sailors and buy new supplies. Although talks took place, it would take decades for the idea to take root.[2]

A First Colony

The first successful attempt to establish a calling station in southern Africa resulted from an accident. In 1647, a Dutch ship named the *Haarlem* was wrecked in Table Bay on the southwest coast of Africa. Its crew went ashore and settled nearby. It took six months for them to be rescued. In the meantime, they got along very well. They grew vegetables and traded with the Khoikhoi who lived in the area for meat. When the men of the *Haarlem* crew returned to the Netherlands in 1649, they spoke very positively about their time in South Africa. Their company decided they had found a good spot to build a place for ships to stop on the route to the Indies.[3]

On June 4, 1652, an expedition led by Jan van Riebeeck reached Table Bay. He had brought with him three ships and one hundred thirty men and women. These settlers had been instructed to build a fort where they could keep a supply of fresh water and grow fruits and vegetables. They were also supposed to establish trade with the Khoikhoi for cattle and sheep, and they were to build a hospital.

The purpose of the settlement was to serve ships that stopped at Table Bay. The colony was sponsored by the Dutch East India Company, not the Dutch government. The government had given the corporation a charter giving it rights over the land in and east of the Cape of Good Hope. The company's establishment of a colony there was a business move, designed to make East Indies trade easier—and more profitable.[4]

The settlers suffered terribly at first. A drought made gardening difficult and led to starvation. The Khoikhoi did not want to trade with the Dutch for animals. Within weeks, fifteen white settlers had died. Half of those who survived were so sick from dysentery, a terrible disease of the lower intestine, that they could not work. Soon, however, the situation improved. The settlers were able to trade for both meat and vegetables. Within fifty years, these white colonists, who would become known as Boers or Afrikaners, had begun to develop their own language, called Afrikaans. In 1657, the Dutch East India Company imported twelve slaves to do hard labor for settlers, such as clearing fields and building.[5] Slavery then increased at a rapid rate.

Slaves were brought in on ships. Some were from other parts of Africa, but many were from Madagascar, Indonesia, India, and Ceylon. The company used slaves to build roads and do other public works. Officials and well-to-do people came to depend on slaves to work in their houses, get wood and water, and plant gardens. Slaves worked in the fields on farms and plantations. By 1708, there were more than one thousand slaves in the colony. In 1793, the population of South Africa was 30,000. Of that number, 14,747 were slaves.

At the beginning of the colonial era, there were some free blacks in the colony. Some slaves had been freed. But this would happen less often as time went by. Slavery would continue in the colony for more than one hundred fifty years.

By 1800, the colony that had begun at Table Bay had greatly expanded. The European population numbered around fifteen thousand.[6] The colony's population included not only Afrikaners and slaves but many other people whom the whites called Coloured. These people included those who had both black and white ancestors.

When the Dutch settlers first arrived in 1652, the African natives were not particularly affected by them. The colonists treated the natives in a friendly manner so that they would trade cattle.

At first, there was also enough land to share. After the Dutch were able to raise their own livestock, however, they no longer needed to treat the native Khoikhoi people carefully. White colonists began to try to push the natives off their land in order to expand the Dutch colony.

First, white farmers would move beyond the colony's boundaries, looking for new land that had water and was easy to plow. Once they had set down roots, the colonial government would then make the land they had taken over part of the colony. The settlers did meet resistance, but they won many of the fights they had with the native Bushmen and Khoikhoi who were defending the land the Dutch wanted to take. The Dutch had many guns. The natives had just the small number of firearms the Dutch had traded them. The Khoikhoi also suffered terribly during a smallpox epidemic in 1713. Many native people agreed to move in order to avoid further contact with the Europeans.[7]

When expansion continued onto their lands, Bantu speakers such as the Xhosa people fought to keep their land. Both sides would suffer deaths in fighting between Afrikaners and natives in 1779 and 1793.

The British Arrive

In 1794, the Dutch East India Company declared bankruptcy, after years of struggling with money troubles. The British saw this as their chance to take over the colony in South Africa. The Dutch who had settled there wanted to stay and rule the colony they had started, but in 1795, British troops captured the Cape Colony, as the Dutch settlement was known. The Dutch briefly won back the colony in 1803, but that would last for only a short time. The British Navy sent sixty-one warships to recapture the Cape Colony in 1806.[8] Meanwhile, the Xhosa people had been fighting the white colonists once more, trying to avoid giving up their land. In 1803, the Xhosa defeated the Afrikaners.

After the British took over the Cape Colony in 1806, British government officials arrived to govern. The governor acknowledged the Khoikhoi as residents of the colony, but also established constraints for them. The natives were not regarded as slaves, but apprentices. In order to move about, they had to get passes from their employers or the farmers whose land they worked.[9]

The first British settlers arrived in 1820. The Xhosa continued to challenge white settlers along the colony's borders. In 1834, the Karrir War took place. Both sides had been making raids, stealing cattle from the enemy. This, however, became a full-scale war in which many people died. The Xhosa finally won.

After the war, the colony's governor started a new province. The government reached an agreement with Xhosa chiefs in which the Xhosa were allowed to live in the white-governed province. In exchange, the Xhosa had to become British subjects and give up their weapons.[10]

Throughout this period, the European settlers generally looked upon native Africans as an inferior race of people, worthy only to serve and work for white men. However, missionaries—religious people who came to the colony to try to convert the natives to Christianity—pressured the British government of the area to grant Africans rights. They succeeded in 1828.

The 50th Ordinance was passed. It granted civil rights to free nonwhites.[11]

The Dutch Break off

By this time, settlers of Dutch descent had become very unhappy with the British government that now ruled the South African colony. Ever since the days of the Dutch East India Company, the Afrikaners had forced slaves to work in their fields and their houses. In 1833, however, the British Parliament in London ruled that all slaves in the British Empire—including those in South Africa—had to be freed.

Afrikaners were extremely angry at this news. They were upset, too, when Parliament made English the colony's official language. Then, an official in Great Britain decided that the colony's governor should not have created the new province, meaning that the land taken from natives would have to be given back. The Dutch regarded this as a final blow.

By 1836, the Afrikaners had begun to move out of the colony and into the land that had been turned back over to native Africans. This migration became known as the Great Trek. Those who took part in it were called *trekboers*. Settlers traveled north and east in several groups, along three routes.

Along the way, they met natives who were willing to fight for their land and their way of life. The Zulu of an area called Natal fought especially ferociously. However, trekkers finally defeated them and received a large part of the Natal district as a result. In other

The native people tried to preserve their traditional way of life as much as possible, despite European interference, maintaining loyalty to local government figures, such as this Zulu chief.

areas, trekkers found unpopulated land on which to settle. In most cases, former inhabitants had died or had been forced to flee during their own native wars with the Zulu.[12]

The trekkers established the Republic of Natal. From the beginning, the native black population was much larger than the white population in Natal. In 1845, the British declared that Great Britain owned the Republic. The colonial government then established reserves—blocks of land the government set aside as places only blacks could live. This left good land free for white settlers. Reserves would soon be established elsewhere, too.

Throughout the colonial history of South Africa, the government would leave tribal chiefs in place to govern their own people. As a result, natives continued to hope that the Europeans would someday leave. In the middle of the nineteenth century, for example, one year the Xhosa killed their cattle and planted no crops, hoping to upset their ancestors enough to make them rise from the dead and chase the white settlers into the sea.[13]

In reaction to the British takeover of Natal, the Dutch fled and moved with other trekkers to the area between the Orange and the Vaal rivers.[14] There, they established another independent nation, known as the South African Republic, or Transvaal. Trekkers also set up the Orange Free State in 1854. Soon, in-fighting caused Afrikaners to establish three more tiny republics, bringing the total of their republics to five.

By this time, the British had three separate colonies in what would later become South Africa: Cape Colony, Natal, and British Kaffraria. Eventually, all these political units—both Afrikaners and British—would unite to become the modern nation of South Africa.

In the 1860s, the British started to bring Indian laborers to their southern Africa plantations. Indians soon came to make up a significant portion of the South African population.

In the 1860s and 1870s, the affairs of the Afrikaners' South African Republic were in an uproar. A president had been forced to step down. The British decided that the country was weak.

In 1877, without the Afrikaners' agreement, the British annexed the South African Republic. This action caused a great feeling of nationalism to begin among the Dutch settlers. In 1880, the Transvaal War of Independence began. Afrikaners defeated British soldiers at the Battle of Majuba Hills on February 27, 1881. However, peace did not come right away. Six months later, the British granted Afrikaners the right to govern Transvaal as long as they accepted British overrule. In other words, Transvaal became a British colony ruled locally by Afrikaners.[15]

In the meantime, a new player—Germany—had arrived on the scene in southern Africa. After Germany formed in 1871, it also wanted to expand. German settlers began to emigrate to Africa. Eventually, Germans ruled East Africa (which would

The Transvaal War was fought when Afrikaners tried to oust British authorities from the area they considered theirs.

later become Tanzania), Cameroon, and the new South West Africa.

One reason so many European powers were interested in controlling this area of the world was that diamonds had been discovered in South Africa in 1870. Interest only increased after gold was discovered in 1885.[16]

The British Build Their Empire

In 1890, Cecil Rhodes became prime minister of the Cape Colony. At first, Rhodes wanted Great Britain to rule all of Africa. Later, he would come to believe that South Africans should be allowed self-rule.

In 1895, Rhodes had been shipping arms to British settlers in Transvaal, who were planning a rebellion against the area's Dutch government. At the same time, he ordered a British settler named Dr. Leander Jameson to invade the Transvaal. Jameson was captured, however, and the British residents of Transvaal did not rebel. Transvaal remained Dutch. Rhodes was forced to resign. The Orange Free State and the Transvaal then decided to fight the British together.

The Boer War

What the British called the Boer War then broke out. (Afrikaners called it the Second War of Freedom.) Today, historians generally call it the South African War. In October 1899, Paul Kruger, the president of Transvaal, notified the British that he wanted their troops to move away from Transvaal's border. When the British did not obey, fighting broke out.

Cecil Rhodes, one of the most influential figures in South African history, was a Cape Colony prime minister who eventually came to believe South Africa should be independent of Great Britain.

Source Document

Words could not portray the scene of misery. The best thing I can do is to ask you to fancy five or six hundred human frameworks of both sexes and all ages, from the tender infant upwards, dressed in the remains of tattered rags, standing in lines, each holding an old blackened can or beef tin, awaiting turn to crawl painfully to the kitchen where the food was distributed. Having obtained the horse soup, fancy them tottering off a few yards and sitting down to wolf up the life-fastening mess, and lick the tins when they had finished. It was one of the most heart-rending sights I had ever witnessed, and I have seen many. . . .[17]

J. E. Neilly was serving in Africa during the Boer War. He recorded the terrible suffering of the native people at Mafeking.

The Afrikaners were better prepared for war than the British were. They did well at first. However, the British had many more troops available.

The Afrikaners suffered terribly during the fighting, which ranged over Transvaal, the Orange Free State, Natal, Zululand, and the Cape Colony. The British government adopted a "scorched earth policy."[18] It ordered the burning of Afrikaner crops and homes and sent the thousands of people left with no place to live to concentration, or prison, camps. More than twenty thousand Afrikaners—mostly women and children—died of disease there.

The war also took a tremendous toll on black South Africans. Estimates of the number of blacks who fought for the British are as high as thirty thousand. More than one hundred thousand blacks who had been living under the Afrikaner government also ended up in concentration camps.[19]

The war finally ended when British and Afrikaner representatives signed the Peace of Vereeniging on May 21, 1902. The Boer republics became British colonies. However, the British promised that the Afrikaners could soon run their own local governments again. The treaty guaranteed that most of those who had fought for the Afrikaners would not be treated as traitors or punished for having fought against the British. Those who were accused of and tried for having committed war crimes were assured that they would not receive a death sentence. The British even agreed to give the Afrikaners £3 million (British currency) to pay off the former republics' war debts. The British government also provided food and other necessities for the Afrikaners and recognized their property rights.

The treaty did not, however, provide as well for the blacks who were living in the republics. Lord Alfred Milner, the reform-minded British administrator involved in the negotiations, wanted very much for

Many European soldiers were killed in the Boer War, but the suffering was especially hard for native Africans, who faced poverty and hunger during the conflict.

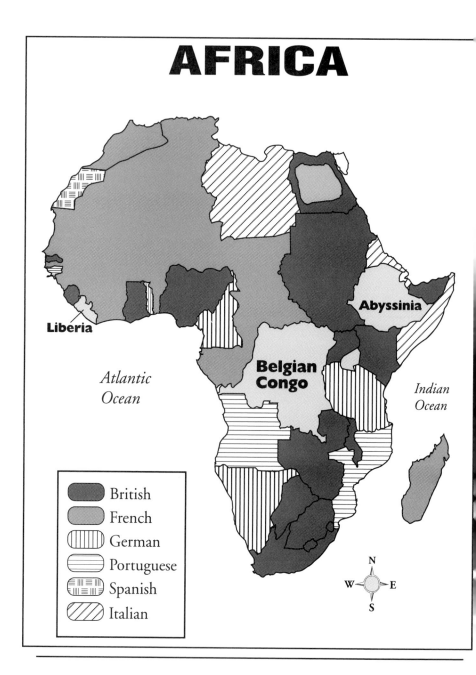

AFRICA

Abyssinia

Liberia

*Atlantic
Ocean*

Belgian
Congo

*Indian
Ocean*

British
French
German
Portuguese
Spanish
Italian

N
W—E
S

By the beginning of the twentieth century, European countries
controlled almost all of the African continent.

blacks living in southern Africa to have the right to vote. However, he did not dare insist that this right be included in the treaty. He feared it would cause Afrikaners and some British settlers to refuse to sign the treaty. In fact, the final surrender document stated outright that blacks would not be given the right to vote before self-government was established in the former republics.

A United South Africa

At the time the treaty was signed, it was unclear what would happen next. Great Britain now had authority over four colonies in southern Africa. No one could tell whether they would eventually unite. If they did, it was unclear whether the British would order it or whether residents themselves would make it happen.

South Africa unified through a slow process that took from 1902 to 1910 to complete. One thing that helped push the colonies of South Africa toward unification was the election of a new government in Great Britain in 1906, which granted self-government to the Transvaal and the Orange River Colony. In May 1908, British and Afrikaners met at a conference, where they began to talk about making the four colonies into one independent country.

Another conference was held that winter. At it, representatives agreed that a single lawmaking authority should be established to rule all of South Africa. A constitution was drafted. After the colonies agreed to accept it, the British Parliament passed the

South Africa Act, the law that made the several colonies of South Africa into one independent country. Formally named the Union of South Africa, it came into being in May 1910.

White South Africans rejoiced. For black South Africans, however, this was not a time of hope. In 1911, the total population of South Africa was 6 million. White people numbered 1.3 million. About two thirds of them were Afrikaners. There were 4 million blacks. The population also included half a million Coloured people and 200,000 Indians.[20]

The Union Constitution spelled out a native policy. It had been approved by extremist Afrikaners, those who were most interested in seeing black South Africans treated differently from white South Africans. The Constitution made sure the new country's society would be a segregated one. The Afrikaners had triumphed.

In the new country, laws would make blacks inferior while white people would enjoy special privileges just because of their race. For example, only a few black people would be allowed to vote. The former republics of Transvaal and the Orange Free State had allowed only white men to vote. This remained the same when they became provinces of South Africa. A few blacks had been able to vote in Natal (economic criteria determined who could vote there). The Cape Colony's policy had been to allow anyone to vote as long as they could read and write and had a large income or owned a house and land outside of the

The South African Parliament, which met in this building in Cape Town, was responsible for instituting the early policies that led to the system of apartheid.

blacks' reserves. These policies continued in South Africa. In the new country, only white men could serve in Parliament. In Natal and the Cape province, blacks were allowed to vote if they met the strict requirements, but few could do so.[21]

Over the decades that followed, segregation would increase. Laws would say where black South Africans could live, what schools they could attend, and what jobs they could hold. They would have little freedom.

After 1948, a new, stronger system of segregation, called apartheid, emerged. It imposed severe oppression on black South Africans that would end only after a long, hard struggle led in part by Nelson Mandela.

Chapter 3

Background of a Freedom Fighter

At birth, the man later called Nelson Mandela was given the first name Rolihlahla. In his native Xhosa language, Rolihlahla means pulling the branch of a tree. Its slang meaning is troublemaker.[1]

Rolihlahla Mandela is a member of the Thembu tribe. There are many tribes and clans that live in South Africa. Many Americans know very little of their family's history. They may not even know when their ancestors arrived in the United States. But like many black South Africans, Mandela was raised to know a lot about his heritage.[2] He can trace his family tree back for centuries. As a child, he learned the stories of the Thembu tribe, which traces its history back for twenty generations. They regard a king named Zwide as their patriarch.

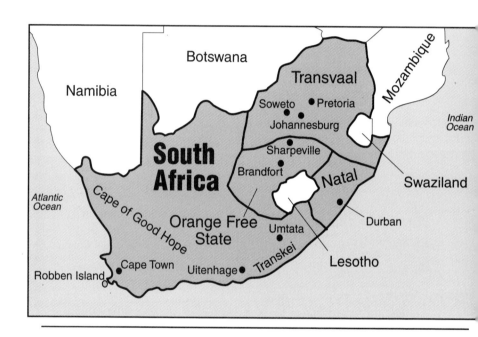

This map shows the area in which Nelson Mandela grew up, and some of the places that would be important to him as he became a freedom fighter.

In the sixteenth century, the Thembu tribe moved from the foothills of the Drakensberg Mountains toward the southeast coast. There, they joined the Xhosa nation. The Xhosas had reached the upper reaches of the Umzimvubu River as early as A.D. 1300. The Xhosa people speak forms of the Bantu language.

Mandela's family belongs to the Madiba clan, founded by a man named Madiba, who ruled in the Transkei in the eighteenth century. Black South Africans sometimes refer to Mandela as Madiba, as a mark of respect.[3]

Birth

Rolihlahla Mandela was born on July 18, 1918, an important time in world history. It was the year World War I ended and the year an influenza epidemic would kill millions worldwide. At the time of his birth, the unified country of South Africa had existed for only eight years.

Rolihlahla's father was named Gadla Henry Mphakanyiswa. Like other men in his own and other South African tribes, Gadla Henry Mphakanyiswa had several wives. Nosekeni Fanny, Rolihlahla's mother, was the third of four women he married. Altogether his father would have thirteen children. Rolihlahla was the youngest of his father's four sons and the first of his mother's four children.

Rolihlahla Mandela was born on his mother's homestead in a tiny village called Mvezo. Mvezo is located on the banks of the Mbashe River in the district of Umtata. Umtata is part of the Transkei territory. Rolihlahla lived there during his childhood. He saw his father only once in a while, because his father traveled between his wives' homesteads. They lived many miles apart. Nevertheless, Rolihlahla and his father were close: Black South African men were generally devoted fathers even when they did not live full-time with their children.[4]

Son of a Chief

When Rolihlahla was born, his father was a chief. The Thembu people had awarded him this status both because of his ancestry and because he had great intelligence and leadership skills.

For centuries, the native blacks of southern Africa had built their society around kings. Kings, however, did not hold absolute power. They took advice from clan heads or chiefs who ranked below them. As a clan chief, Rolihlahla's father was an extremely important counselor to two kings. Gadla Henry Mphakanyiswa could not read or write, but he knew his people's history and was a persuasive speaker. He played a very important part in government meetings.

At the time of Rolihlahla's birth, conditions were changing for black South Africans. Before the country united, they had enjoyed more political rights. After unification, the British government claimed the right to confirm all appointments of tribal authorities. The Union of South Africa soon began to follow a general native policy that hurt blacks and other people of color in other ways as well.

In 1911, the Mines and Works Act said that black South Africans could no longer work in skilled jobs without special permission from the government. They would be forced to do hard labor, such as working in the mines and on the railroads. Blacks needed special permission to work at office jobs or in stores. In 1913, the Natives' Land Act said rural black South Africans could live on just 7.3 percent of the land designated as reserves for them.

These were the first of many laws passed to segregate South Africa. They took effect slowly. In 1923, the Urban Areas Act stated blacks would have to leave their homes in cities. From that point on, blacks were supposed to live in segregated communities on the cities' outskirts. They would be allowed to enter cities only "to minister to the white man's need."[5]

Many black South Africans fought back against the segregation. Some white South Africans protested segregation, too. Mandela's father, Gadla Henry Mphakanyiswa, would become militant. When Rolihlahla was still very young, his father received an order to appear before the local magistrate, a representative of the British government. He sent back a message that said, "I will not come, I am still girding for battle."[6] In doing so, he was showing that he did not believe he needed to obey the laws of the British government. He followed the customs of his own people, instead. In response, the magistrate stripped

Segregation laws made it impossible for most native blacks to find many different types of jobs. Most Africans were restricted to working in such occupations as mining.

him of his position as chief. He would no longer receive a salary from the government. The government also took away most of his land and his animals. His entire family suffered from the loss of his fortune and title.

Forced to Move

After Gadla Henry Mphakanyiswa was removed from office, Nosekeni Fanny, Rolihlahla's mother, and her children had to leave her homestead. She moved from Mvezo to Qunu, a village where she had friends and relations who could help support her children. Qunu was located in a grassy, well-watered valley. It had a population of a few hundred people. There, everybody lived in a cluster of huts with mud walls and grass roofs.

In town, there were two small schools for little children and a general store. Outside of the village were fields, where women raised maize (corn) and pastures where cattle, sheep, goats, and horses grazed. Most of the year, the village's men were away, working on white men's farms or in mines. They usually returned twice a year to plow. Women and children hoed, weeded, and harvested the crops. The residents did not own their land. Almost no black South Africans owned their own property. The law required them to rent the land they farmed from the national government.

In Qunu, Nosekeni Fanny had three huts. She used one for storage, one for cooking, and one for sleeping. Nelson Mandela later remembered the huts always

43

being crowded with children. He could not remember ever being alone. His extended family was extremely tight-knit. He spent as much time with his aunts and uncles as with his parents and he thought of his cousins as brothers and sisters. When he was very young, he spent his days playing in the grass that surrounded his village. When he was five, he became a herd boy, tending calves and sheep.

He had time to swim and fish and to hunt birds with a slingshot. He learned how to gather food such as honey, fruit, and roots. He fought with sticks with his friends. The boys also played *thinti*—a game where one team uses sticks to try to knock down another team's target while defending its own.

At night, he went back to his mother's hut. While she cooked the evening meal, she would tell the children stories. Through these tales and observations, Mandela learned about his family tree and Xhosa custom, ritual, and taboos. (Taboos are a culture's banned behaviors. For example, most cultures consider it taboo to marry one's sister or brother.)

During his life at Qunu, Rolihlahla saw just a few white men. The local government official was white, as was the owner of the nearest store. Having learned from the actions of his elders, Rolihlahla later said, "I was aware that [whites] were to be treated with a mixture of fear and respect. But their role in my life was a distant one, and I thought little if at all about the white man in general or relations between my own people and these curious and remote figures."[7] He did, however, meet other black people who were not part of the Xhosa tribe.

Education

Rolihlahla's father followed the beliefs of his tribe's traditional religion, worshiping the god Qamata. His mother, on the other hand, met two brothers, members of another clan that also lived in the area, and heard them talk about their Christian faith. She converted to Christianity. Rolihlahla was baptized as a Methodist.

At the age of seven, he was sent to a Christian school. He was the first member of his family ever to attend school. In those days, only one of about seven black South African children went to school.[8] On his first day there, his teacher gave him a new English name, Nelson, by which white people would call him from then on. Teachers at the school gave every black student an English name.

His Father's Death

One night in 1927, when Rolihlahla was nine, his father arrived unexpectedly. He was making regular rounds of his wives' homes. But this time he came a few days earlier than expected.

When Rolihlahla realized that his father had arrived, he rushed to see him. He found his father lying down, in the middle of a terrible coughing fit. "Even to my young eyes, it was clear that my father was not long for this world. He was ill with some type of lung disease, but it was not diagnosed, as my father had never visited a doctor," Mandela later remembered.[9]

Gadla Henry Mphakanyiswa stayed with Rolihlahla and his mother for several days. He neither moved nor spoke. Finally, one night, he asked for his pipe. Within an hour, he died, with his pipe still lit.

Nelson Mandela later remembered that, after his father died, he felt "cut adrift," as though he had lost his anchor. His father played a huge role in his life. "Although my mother was the center of my existence, I defined myself through my father," he later wrote.[10]

Life With Jongintaba

After a short time of mourning, Rolihlahla's mother decided that it was time for her son to leave Qunu. He never even asked where he would go or why he was being sent away. He was too stunned to protest. He and his mother set off on foot, carrying the few things he owned. They walked west all day. It was a hard trip. The dirt roads they walked on were rocky. Finally, late in the day, they arrived at a village built around a large house, the fanciest he had ever seen. It was the royal residence of the regent, or king, Jongintaba Dalindyebo. Rolihlahla's father had been an advisor to Jongintaba.

About twenty tribal elders were sitting in the shade near the doorway of Jongintaba's main house. Suddenly, a car came in through the gate. Everybody jumped to their feet, shouting, "Hail, Jongintaba." Nelson Mandela always remembered the impression made by the man who stepped out. A short, heavy man, he wore an elegant suit and carried himself with confidence. Mandela desperately wanted to be part of Jongintaba's world. "Until then . . . ," he remembered, "I had no thought of money, or class, or fame, or power. Suddenly a new world opened before me."[11]

Later, Nelson Mandela found out why his mother had brought him there. When he had learned of Nelson's father's death, Jongintaba had offered to become Mandela's guardian. Mandela's mother had agreed. Mandela essentially became an adopted son to the king. Jongintaba and his wife, No England, acted as his parents. They advised him, scolded him, and cared for him.

A New Life

Living with the king, Nelson Mandela went to a new school. There, he received a much better education than at the school in Qunu. He studied English, the Xhosa language, history, and geography. He did well and worked very hard.

He also made new friends, especially with Jongintaba's children. Like them, in his spare time, he worked as a plowboy. Sometimes he herded animals or guided wagons. He rode horses and used slingshots to shoot birds.

In his new home, he got to see a much more Westernized culture than he had in Qunu. The blacks in Mqhekezweni had more contact with whites and lived in a similar fashion. Now Mandela wore modern

Western clothes. He went to the local Methodist church. He lived for the first time in quite luxurious houses like those built in Europe and the United States.

He also had a chance to watch his foster father at work. Periodically, the king presided over tribal meetings, where any man interested could come and debate an issue. Meetings ended only when the entire group had reached some kind of agreement. Mandela believed he was watching true democracy at work.

He soon came to know his tribe's chiefs and headmen. At first, when they realized he was listening to them tell stories about Xhosa history, they shooed him away. But gradually, they came to accept and include him. In the end, Mandela was treated with respect by the men in his foster father's circle.

Becoming an Adult

At the age of sixteen, Mandela, his foster brother Justice, and twenty-five other boys took part in circumcision ritual ceremonies that signaled their entry into adulthood. Friends and family gave the young men presents. Mandela received two cows and four sheep.

At first, it was a very happy day for him. However, his mood changed when he listened to the main ceremony speaker, who discussed blacks' treatment at the hands of white South Africans. Nelson Mandela remembered thinking at the time that the speaker was foolish. As a young man, Mandela still saw whites as benefactors. Later, Mandela would develop very different opinions.

Away to School

At this point, Jongintaba sent Mandela away to school. His education was considered very important. When he grew up, his foster family planned for Mandela to become a counselor to Jongintaba's son, who would be the next king.

First, Mandela attended Clarkebury boarding school. Jongintaba himself drove Mandela to the school, which was run for black children by a white Methodist minister. It was a large place, with more than twenty buildings, all in the colonial or European style.

There, Mandela took classes from teachers who had studied at a university. After classes, he worked in the principal's garden. At Clarkebury, Mandela finished in two years the full course of education that usually took three years. He was a hard worker.

In 1937, Mandela went on to a junior college at Healdtown, where he spent two years. Mandela, like his adopted father's other sons, received an exceptional education for a black child. Jongintaba took advantage of all the opportunities South Africa's segregated society would allow his children.

On to the University

After Mandela completed his studies at Healdtown in 1939, Jongintaba decided he should go on to the University College of Fort Hare. It was then the only

Nelson Mandela could not have realized during his youth that he would one day be the leader of the South African nation.

residential college black South Africans were allowed to attend. To scholars from the United States or Europe, Fort Hare, with its enrollment of just one hundred fifty students, would have seemed very small. Its student body was made up mostly of blacks not just from South Africa but from elsewhere in Africa. There were also Asian students and people of mixed ancestry there. There were no white students.

While at Fort Hare, Mandela lived in a house owned by the Methodist church on the edge of campus. Never before had he seen so many modern conveniences, including flush toilets and hot showers. In his spare time, he attended church, played soccer, and ran for the cross-country team. He also enjoyed an active social life. He loved to dance, which made him popular with young women.[12]

In his first year of college, he took classes in English, anthropology, politics, native administration, and Roman Dutch law. He did well in his studies, but he was not an outstanding student.

Immediately, he got involved in campus politics. He was elected to his dormitory's House Committee, whose members were traditionally upperclassmen. At the same time, he became interested in world affairs. In 1939, South Africa joined World War II on the side of the Allies—Great Britain, France, the Soviet Union, and later, the United States—after Jan Christiaan Smuts, a South African Army general and long-time politician, became the country's prime minister. Every

WORLD WAR II IN EUROPE

- Axis countries
- Allied countries
- Neutral countries

World War II not only divided the nations of Europe, but also included the European colonies in Africa.

day, Mandela read about South African war efforts and developments in Europe and Japan.

When he first arrived at college, Nelson Mandela's goal was to work in the government's Native Affairs Department. He wanted to be a civil servant. At that time, this department still played a somewhat protective role toward blacks and other people of color. It tried to make sure they obeyed the laws that governed their lives.[13]

All through his first year, his goal remained the same. Thinking about the future, he hoped to become part of South Africa's bureaucracy. He expected South African blacks' situation to remain in the future pretty much the same as it was then. What he and many others failed to realize was that the situation would, in fact, change very quickly. Apartheid was about to begin. It would turn Mandela, the hopeful young college student, into an activist known throughout the world.

Chapter 4

The Roots of Apartheid

Nelson Mandela grew up in a segregated society. During his youth, segregation existed not just in South Africa, but elsewhere in Africa, Asia, the Caribbean, and the United States. In many places around the world, laws forced blacks to use separate facilities and attend separate schools.

South African Society

In the years following the creation of South Africa in 1910, whites combined their power. The white population of South Africa remained divided into two separate groups: the English-speakers, who had originally come from Great Britain, and the Afrikaners, who were descended from South Africa's Dutch colonists. At first, most of the country's leaders were English-speakers. They played an important role in the South African economy, ruling the business world. Afrikaners generally worked in agriculture. Although they had less power, however, they made up most of the voting body. Black South Africans, who made up the majority of the population, had virtually no power. They were legally oppressed and could not usually vote.

South African Politics

The South African political party won the country's first general election, held in 1910. It was led by Louis Botha and Jan Christiaan Smuts, both of whom were Afrikaners. They both believed in coalition, saying that Afrikaners had to cooperate with English-speakers. They also accepted South Africa's membership in the British Empire.

Upon hearing these views, many Afrikaners believed Botha and Smuts had sold out. Some became so upset that they no longer wanted Botha and Smuts as leaders. These Afrikaners formed a new political party, the National party, in 1914. Poor Afrikaners, as well as intellectuals, joined the Nationalists. They fought to protect Afrikaners' interests in particular. They wanted South Africa to withdraw from the British Empire.

During World War I (1914–1918), some Afrikaners hoped to regain their independence from British rule. But the government put down their armed rebellion. South African soldiers also fought German troops in East Africa and South West Africa. After the war,

Jan Christiaan Smuts (in car at front) became one of the most controversial South African leaders.

mine owners wanted to replace some semi-skilled white workers with blacks, whom they could pay much less. The white union went on strike. The government finally settled the matter by declaring martial law and using weapons, including tanks and machine guns.

After this, Afrikaners were so angry that they refused to vote for Smuts's party. The Nationalists, led by J.B.M. Hertzog, won the election of 1924. The new government passed more laws favoring whites in general and Afrikaners in particular. It also fought for autonomy, or less interference in its affairs, from Great Britain.

English and Dutch had been the official languages of the country. In 1925, Afrikaans replaced Dutch as an official language. By 1931, South Africa had begun to act on its own on the world scene. It had its own diplomats.

The Great Depression—a worldwide economic recession that caused terrible poverty and suffering—really hurt South Africa. With the economy in serious trouble, the two major political parties—Smuts's South African party and Hertzog's National party—reached an agreement. A coalition government formed. Members of both parties played important leadership roles. In 1934, the United party was created out of the combined South African and National parties. Smaller political parties also formed. Now the Afrikaners, who believed strongly in preventing "mixing of the races," gained even more power.[1]

In 1939, trouble erupted for the new United party. Great Britain had declared its intentions to fight Adolf Hitler's Nazi Germany in what would become World War II. Hertzog and his followers wanted South Africa to remain neutral during the war. Smuts and his followers, however, wanted to join the war on the side of Allies—Great Britain, France, the Soviet Union, and later, the United States. The South African Parliament finally voted to declare war on Germany, but by only a small margin. Hertzog demanded that the government be dissolved and new elections held. The governor-general refused to let this happen. Hertzog then resigned as prime minister, and Smuts stepped back into the office.

Segregation

In the meantime, segregation continued to divide South African society. The Natives Land Act of 1913 had set aside just 22 million acres as reserves for black South Africans to live on. However, the South African Native Trust was given authority to buy more land later. By 1939, reserves took up 11.7 percent of the total area of South Africa. The land the black South Africans were forced to live on and farm was generally poor.

As of 1925, black South African men had to pay a poll tax if they wanted to vote. Eventually, black farming collapsed. Black South Africans could no longer feed themselves, and their quality of life fell apart.

Unable to support their families through farming, the men who lived on the reserves got jobs working for whites on farms or in the mines or industry.

By 1936, the urban population of South Africa numbered 3 million. About a third of the population was black. Seventeen percent of black South Africans lived in towns.[2] Laws were written that dictated where blacks could live inside cities. To prevent more blacks from moving into the city, Parliament wrote pass laws. These forced blacks to get permission from the white farmers they worked for before they could quit and other passes from government officials before they could look for work in a city. Laws prevented black workers from striking and gave white workers most of the skilled jobs.

Resistance Efforts

The South African government made it very difficult for black South Africans to fight segregation. Blacks were armed to help South Africa in World War I but they had to return their weapons when the war ended.

Blacks also found very little support from Indian and Coloured South Africans. Although these other ethnic groups also faced discrimination in South Africa, it was generally less severe than that against blacks. Black families broke up when their men were forced to leave the reserves to work. This made the black population weak. It also disrupted traditional forms of black government—the young black men who left reserves to find work stopped seeing tribal leaders as authority figures.[3]

Three political organizations were founded to try to improve the lives of those groups facing segregation in South Africa. Coloureds founded the African Political Organization, Indians formed the South African Indian Congress, and in 1912, blacks founded the South African Native National Congress. This last group would later be called the African National Congress (ANC).

The constitution of the ANC specifically stated that it would work within the law. It listed as its main concerns the "educational, social, economic and political elevation of the native people in South Africa."[4] The ANC's methods were cautious. It mostly protested upcoming laws by lobbying white political leaders.

From time to time, members of all three organizations cooperated. But both together and apart, they failed to win any substantial victories. They were never able to mobilize the masses.

A more radical group, the Industrial and Commercial Worker Union (ICU), was formed in 1919. Protesting unfair conditions, the ICU refused to work, stole livestock, and destroyed property. Eventually, the group's leader was charged with stealing money from the ICU, and after much infighting, the group fell apart.[5] In 1921, white South Africans formed a Communist party, but it remained small.

Source Document

The objects for which the Association is established are: —

To form a National Vigilant Association and a deliberative Assembly or Council, without legislative pretentions;

To unite, absorb, consolidate and preserve under its aegis existing political and educational Associations, Vigilance Committees and other public and private bodies whose aims are the promotion and safeguarding of the interests of the aboriginal races.

To be the medium of expression of representative opinion and to formulate a standard policy on Native Affairs for the benefit and guidance of the Union Government and Parliament;

To educate Parliament and Provincial Councils, Municipalities, other bodies and the public generally regarding the requirements and aspirations of the Native people; and to enlist the sympathy and support of such European Societies, Leagues or Unions as might be willing to espouse the cause of right and fair treatment of coloured races.

To educate Bantu people on their rights, duties and obligations to the state and to themselves individually and collectively; and to promote mutual help, feeling of fellowship and a spirit of brotherhood among them.

To encourage mutual understanding and to bring together into common action as one political people all tribes and clans of various tribes or races and by means of combined effort and united political organisation to defend their freedom, rights and privileges;

To discourage and contend against racialism and tribal feuds or to secure the elimination of racialism and tribal feuds; jealousy and petty quarrels by economic combination, education, goodwill and by other means. . . .[6]

The African National Congress was formed to try to defend the rights of native black Africans. Its constitution outlined its beliefs.

Mandela Becomes Interested in Resistance

In 1940, Mandela returned to Fort Hare to complete his bachelor of arts degree. He got in trouble with university authorities for supporting a student boycott. When he went home for vacation, he told his foster father, Jongintaba, that he was thinking about dropping out of school. His foster father insisted that he return. Mandela decided to let the matter rest for the time being.

A few weeks later, Jongintaba informed his family that he had arranged marriages for his son Justice and for Mandela. Neither young man wanted to get married. But rather than confront Jongintaba, the two young men ran away.

Johannesburg

They arrived in Johannesburg. Mandela considered it a place of great opportunity. The next day, they applied for jobs at the city's biggest gold mine. Justice, Mandela's foster brother, got a good job as a clerk. Mandela became a mine policeman. When Jongintaba found out where they were, he tried to make them come home. They refused.

Soon, Nelson Mandela got a position as a clerk at a large law firm that handled business for both white and black South Africans. At night, he worked on correspondence lessons from the University of South Africa. He wanted to finish his degree and go on to study law.

As a law clerk, Mandela became friends with two Communists. Communist party members hoped that one day they would be able to overthrow the government. Mandela was just beginning to think about the need to force the government to reform. Although Mandela did not join the Communist party, he often went to its meetings and parties. At the same time, Mandela also learned a lot about the ANC.

Toward the end of 1941, Mandela saw his foster father, Jongintaba. Jongintaba expressed approval of Mandela's plans to study law. They parted on good terms.

In the winter of 1942, Jongintaba died. After his funeral, Nelson Mandela returned to Johannesburg alone. Justice took his father's place, serving as the new king.

At the end of 1942, Mandela earned his bachelor's degree. But he continued to work for the law firm. Then he started taking courses part-time at the University of Witwatersrand in Johannesburg, working toward a law degree. At the time, he was the only black student in the law school.[7]

The African National Congress

By this time, Mandela was spending a lot of time with Gaur Radebe, the only other black staff member at the law firm. Radebe took him to meetings of the ANC, and he helped him adopt a PanAfrican point of view. PanAfricans believed that, ultimately, all black South Africans, regardless of what tribe or clan they had been born into, should unite to fight for reform. During this period, Mandela also met Walter Sisulu, a leader of the ANC who would later have even more influence on him than Radebe.

At this time, the ANC was setting new goals. In 1941, British Prime Minister Winston Churchill and United States President Franklin Delano Roosevelt had signed the Atlantic Charter, which supported the rights of all individuals. Africans had been inspired by the charter. Members of the ANC had written their own charter, which they called the African Claims. It demanded full citizenship for all Africans. It also called for blacks to be allowed to own land in South Africa.[8]

The Youth League

In 1943, Mandela often went to Sisulu's house, where ANC members gathered to visit and talk about politics and their cause. Decades later, Sisulu would remember, "When a young man of Nelson's nature came, it was a godsend to me. Because we were looking for people who could finally have influence on the situation in the country."[9] Mandela was intelligent and self-confident, and he would prove himself dedicated.

Mandela became so involved with Sisulu's ANC group that he became a member of a delegation of young men that went to meet with ANC president Dr. A. B. Xuma. They wanted to establish a Youth League for the ANC. They had already drafted a constitution and written a manifesto, outlining the actions they

Apartheid segregated most aspects of South African society, including public facilities such as this sports arena.

wanted to take. Xuma protested, arguing that a youth league should recruit for the ANC and take no action on its own.

After this meeting, a provisional committee of the Youth League formed. Its members attended the ANC National Congress in December 1943. The ANC accepted the proposal for forming the league.

The Youth League began on Easter Sunday, 1944. One hundred young black men attended. That day, the members elected officers. Mandela was elected to the executive committee.

The Youth League members were dedicated to African nationalism. They wanted to unite the various black tribes living in South Africa and overthrow the white government. Eventually, Sisulu and Mandela, in particular, hoped the Youth League would be able to gain control of the entire ANC, forcing it to become a much more radical organization than in the past.[10]

Chapter 5

Apartheid Is Put Into Place

In the 1940s, even as changes were taking place within the ANC, a power shift was occurring on the South African political scene. The National party had been gaining strength, although the United party controlled the government through World War II. In 1948, the Nationalists beat the United party incumbents.

During the campaign, National party candidates talked a lot about the "black danger." They wanted to reinforce segregation. They also wanted to remove missionary influence by closing their schools for blacks. They wanted to take away the small voice blacks had had in South African politics by getting rid of the Natives Representative Council, which was supposed to present natives' concerns to South Africa's Parliament. Laws also discriminated against Coloureds and the large number of Indians who had come to work in South Africa. Nationalists considered them inferior, too.

The Nationalists Legalize Segregation

In office, Nationalists began to pass laws that created a new system called apartheid. *Apartheid* is a term Afrikaners coined, meaning apartness.[1] It would force all nonwhites to live apart from whites.

Apartheid officially began in 1948. Its roots stemmed from the decision Dutch and British officials had made years earlier to keep native Africans, slaves, and Coloured people from having a voice in the colonial government.[2] In the years that followed, the white settlers and their descendants kept control of the government, despite the fact that they made up a minority of the population.

The segregated history of South Africa made it easy for the National party to establish apartheid as a new official government policy. Most blacks were already not allowed to vote. Supporters of apartheid wanted complete racial segregation. They did not, however, want nonwhites to enjoy rights equal to those of whites under a so-called "separate but equal" policy like that of the United States. Instead, they pushed for a society "in which the lighter your skin, the more benefits you received."[3]

There would be four categories in this society: white, Indian, Coloured, and African, or black. Whites generally enjoyed comfortable lives. The government gave them excellent public services, including schools, hospitals, parks, transportation, water, electricity, and sewage.[4] Nonwhites did not get the same public services. Blacks were the most deprived.

Once in power, the Nationalists began to make laws to extend the antiblack customs and traditions that were already in place. The government's goal became "to preserve white power in general—and Afrikaner power in particular."[5]

A great deal of social upheaval followed. The Nationalist government moved quickly to repress nonwhite people. It banned mixed marriages—marriages between whites and nonwhites.

The South African legislature also passed laws that removed anyone who was not an Afrikaner from a position of authority in the government. New laws required all employees in government offices to be able to speak both English and Afrikaans. This meant that not only blacks and other nonwhites but also many white English speakers were forced out of their jobs. Afrikaners who could speak English, as well as their native Afrikaans, got the jobs.

Soon the Nationalist government required every resident of South Africa to be issued an identification card that recorded his or her race. To decide what race a particular person was, officials often used ridiculous measures. For instance, they might push a pencil into a person's hair. If the pencil stayed in, the person would be classified as black and restricted accordingly.[6]

New laws required people to live within their racial category. This meant that many people had to move.

Blacks were forced to live in segregated areas, and men could only enter certain places to work. Despite these restrictions, many families followed the men of their households and set up squatters' camps to be closer to one another.

Laws allowed the government to take the land and property of more than 3 million people.

By 1953, South African law would provide for separate facilities—including post offices, trains, offices, beaches, parks, bus stops, benches, service counters, and elevators—for whites and nonwhites.[7] The lives of all nonwhite South Africans were terribly disrupted by laws that told them where to live and work.

The Effects of Apartheid

Apartheid would mean that Nelson Mandela, like other blacks and nonwhites, had to give up many of his hopes and dreams. When he first went to college, black South Africans were still allowed to work for the government. Apartheid now meant that he faced limits both in how he could earn his living and the type of life he could lead.

In the 1940s, Mandela experienced huge changes in his personal life. He moved from place to place. Several times he lived for weeks or months with Walter Sisulu's family. At his house, he met Sisulu's cousin, Evelyn Mase, who was training to become a nurse and also came from Transkei.

In 1944, Nelson Mandela and Evelyn Mase were married. At first, they lived with her family. In 1946, they had their first child, a son named Madiba Thembekile. Because they had a child, the state let them have a house of their own. It was a tiny house with just two rooms. It was in Orlando West. The neighborhood was filled with hundreds of houses just like theirs. They all had tin roofs and cement floors. None had a flush toilet. A double bed filled up the entire bedroom. There was still no electricity in the neighborhood, so they used kerosene lamps.

For years, Mandela had frequently lived with friends and relations. Now his own house was always filled with visitors. According to the customs of his tribe, all members of his large extended family could expect a welcome. His sister moved in with them so she could attend a local high school.

Nelson Mandela greatly enjoyed family life, but his devotion to his political causes meant he was rarely at home. For the first year of his marriage, he continued to work. In 1947, he left the law firm of Witkin, Sidelsky, and Eidelman to study law full-time at the University of the Witwatersrand. Without a salary, he had to take out a loan from the Bantu Welfare Trust at the South African Institute of Race Relations.

At that time, Evelyn was working. His loan and her salary combined to make enough for the family to live on. Three months later, however, Mandela had to borrow more money because Evelyn was about to go on maternity leave. Their second child was a girl named Makaziwe. From her birth, she was sickly. Her parents took turns staying up with her at night. Even as a nurse, Evelyn could not help the baby get well. Makaziwe died before she was a year old.

Mandela and the Struggle Against Apartheid

From the beginning, many South Africans were against apartheid. White South African churches issued statements against the new system. English-speaking students at white universities opposed apartheid. White women formed a protest group called the Black Sash. The Communist party tried to take away power from the Nationalists. But the ANC's Youth League would be the most vocal protest group.

Mandela remained very involved with the ANC Youth League after his marriage. In 1947, he served on the executive committee of the Transvaal branch of the ANC. In 1948, he served as the Youth League's general secretary.

When apartheid was instituted, Mandela was "stunned and dismayed."[8] One of his friends thought the Nationalists' rise to power would, in the end, help South African blacks. Now they had a common enemy to fight against.

Members of the Youth League became extremely revolutionary. The Youth League issued a call for civil disobedience. Its struggle against the government would last for more than twelve years. By the end of 1949, members of the Youth League had already influenced the ANC as a whole, getting the national conference to endorse a program of action designed to oppose white rule. Under this plan, blacks would refuse to go along with the white government.

In May 1950, the government decided to outlaw the Communist party. The Communists staged a mass labor strike, in protest. At the time, Mandela was against black participation in the strike because it had not been planned by the ANC. He wanted blacks to continue to go to work. However, African workers did go out on strike in force. The day ended in disaster when policemen opened fire on a crowd of black protesters, killing eighteen.[9]

The government then drafted a new law called the Suppression of Communism Act. Under it, any person who tried to bring about change through unlawful acts could be considered a Communist. It banned almost all political protest.

A number of groups, including the ANC, took part in the National Day of Protest on June 26, 1950. Eventually, the alliance forged between the ANC and the Communist party would cause problems within the ANC.

Mandela's participation in anti-apartheid activity was limited by his new job at a law firm. Mandela had to make the tough choice as to which would come first—his politics or his family. Devoted to his beliefs, Mandela continued to put politics ahead of his family. In fact, Mandela worked so hard that he had little time to celebrate the birth of his second son, Makgatho Lewanika. He was thrilled when his efforts had success, but his commitment to politics was becoming all-consuming.

In 1951, Mandela became president of the Youth League. He saw his greatest challenge as maintaining contact between the Youth League and the people. In the years that followed, apartheid would become an important matter to people all over the world, far beyond South Africa.

Defiance Campaign

In 1952, Nelson Mandela was elected president of a branch of the African National Congress—the Transvaal branch, with headquarters in Johannesburg. Mandela was one of four ANC deputy presidents.

At this time, the ANC was going through important changes. In the early days of the ANC, its president, Pixley Seme, had, along with others, insisted that the group remain nonviolent. Seme had been succeeded as president by Alfred Xuma. Xuma had done a lot to strengthen the ANC. Under him, the ANC Youth League had formed. Still, he had continued to stress the need for moderation. He thought that, if the organization acted too early, before the masses of South African people were ready to take part, the government would simply persecute ANC leaders, who would then be unable to get anything done.

The ANC Becomes More Radical

Young ANC leaders like Mandela, Walter Sisulu, and Oliver Tambo, on the other hand, were willing to risk everything to try to bring about change. They did not want to wait to try to negotiate with the government. They were impatient to act.

In 1949, they pushed Xuma out of office by convincing other ANC members not to reelect him. His successor, James Moroka, was elected with their backing. In return, he gave them much more power in the organization. Under their influence, the ANC became committed to what its authors called the Programme of Action, a program of "militant resistance."[1]

Defiance Campaign

The first important step the ANC made under Moroka was to begin to cooperate with the South African Indian Congress (SAIC) and other South Africans who were also fighting apartheid. In 1952, the ANC and the Indian Congress formed the Joint Planning Council. It launched a defiance campaign against the government.

First, Moroka and Walter Sisulu wrote to South African Prime Minister Daniel Malan, asking him to repeal the new discriminatory laws. They said that their people were "fully resolved to achieve [democracy, liberty, and harmony] in our lifetime."[2] Malan replied that the government would not back down and warned that, if troublemakers continued to resist government efforts to segregate South African society, the government would "use the full machinery at its disposal to quell any disturbances."[3]

The ANC decided it was not afraid of Malan's threats, and in conjunction with the Indian Congress, began its Campaign for the Defiance of Unjust Laws. Mandela served as volunteer-in-chief for the campaign. He coordinated the efforts of thousands, finding ways for them to defy the government and scheduling demonstrations.

Some Coloureds joined the campaign. Many of them spoke Afrikaans and had been raised as Afrikaners during the period of segregation. Conditions had significantly worsened for them when apartheid began. Other Coloureds, however, supported the Nationalists.

Following Mandela's instructions, on June 26, 1952, thousands risked prison terms. Blacks and Indians sat on "white only" benches in parks. They broke government-imposed curfews. In businesses and offices, they went up to desks that were supposed to serve only whites. A white sympathizer broke the law by entering a black township without permission.

Protesters continued their acts of defiance into December 1952. Eventually, the government arrested some eight thousand participants in the campaign.

In October 1952, the nature of the campaign changed. Violence broke out among protesters for the first time. Both blacks and whites, protesting violence, rioted. Police broke up these protests with force. On November 10, police stormed a prayer meeting sponsored by the ANC, despite the fact that its organizers had permission from police to hold the meeting. Policemen fixed bayonets to the ends of their rifles and charged at those who had gathered to pray together for the end of apartheid.

The ANC finally stopped the defiance campaign because the government had significantly increased penalties. In one way, the campaign had cost its supporters dearly. Fourteen protesters had died and another thirty-five were wounded at the hands of police.

On the other hand, the ANC had succeeded in packing the prisons. It had also succeeded by gaining ninety-three thousand new dues-paying members. Its membership had swelled from seven thousand to one hundred thousand by the end of the campaign.

Arrest

In the middle of the campaign, on July 30, 1952, twenty-one of its leaders were arrested, including Mandela. After being released on bail, they went back to work on the campaign. They all went on trial in September.

The public held rallies in the street to demonstrate support for them. During the trial, the ANC president hired his own attorney and publicly denounced the cause.

In December, the judge found every defendant guilty. He sentenced them to nine months of imprisonment at hard labor but suspended the sentence for two years. In his closing statements, the judge said that, while they had broken the law, he regarded them as examples of nonviolence.

During this period, Mandela made a bold professional move. He opened his own law office in August 1952. He became partners with Oliver Tambo, whom he had known since his days at Fort Hare and who was also involved in the ANC.

Theirs was the only all-black firm then in South Africa. Often they represented blacks who had been arrested for breaking apartheid laws. In fact, they had to break the law in order to keep their office in the city.

New ANC Campaigns

After the defiance campaign trial, ANC leaders were harassed by police and government officials. The government said they could not attend political meetings. If they did so, they would be arrested. Forbidden to call mass meetings, issue press statements, or publish leaflets, ANC leaders had to come up with new ways to stir people to action.

One new protest method they used was a boycott of black schools. Recently, the government had created the new Bantu education system. No longer could black children go to schools run by churches or missionaries.[4] Mandela and other ANC leaders believed the new public education was so inferior that they asked black families not to let their children go to the schools the government ran for black children.

In September 1953, the government ordered Mandela to give up his place in the ANC. Working from behind the scenes, he helped organize the Congress of the People. Members of the ANC, the South African Indian Congress, the South African Coloured People's Organization, the Congress of Democrats (a group of antigovernment whites), and the South African Congress of Trade Unions sent three thousand delegates to the congress. It issued a document called the Freedom Charter. It was moderate in tone, including little more than statements such as, "All shall be equal before the law!" The government considered it very subversive.[5]

The ANC Faces Charges Again

On December 5, 1956, the government ordered 156 people, including Nelson Mandela, arrested and charged with high treason. The trial would last for more than four years. During that period, Mandela and his codefendants were free on bail. They went about their daily lives, but had the threat of imprisonment always over their heads.

During this period, Mandela and his wife, Evelyn, grew apart because he devoted so little time to his family. They were divorced in 1957. In the meantime, Mandela started a new romance with Winnie Nomzano Madikizela, a social worker. She understood from the

Source Document

We, the People of South Africa, declare for all our country and the world to know:

that South Africa belongs to all who live in it, black and white, and that no government can justly claim authority unless it is based on the will of all the people;

that our people have been robbed of their birthright to land, liberty and peace by a form of government founded on injustice and inequality;

that our country will never be prosperous or free until all our people live in brotherhood, enjoying equal rights and opportunities;

that only a democratic state, based on the will of all the people, can secure to all their birthright without distinction of colour, race, sex or belief;

And therefore, we, the people of South Africa, black and white together equals, countrymen and brothers adopt this Freedom Charter;

And we pledge ourselves to strive together, sparing neither strength nor courage, until the democratic changes here set out have been won. . . .[6]

The Freedom Charter demanded equality for black Africans, based on human rights theories.

beginning that they could never lead an ordinary life. Mandela would always spend most of his time fighting apartheid. They were married on June 14, 1958.

Sharpeville Massacre

In the late 1950s, the ANC split. Some African nationalists had been complaining that the ANC was not doing enough to fight apartheid. This was largely because many of the ANC's more radical leaders were in prison.

On April 6, 1959, three hundred former members of the ANC, led by Robert Mangaliso Sobukwe, founded a new group. It was called the Pan-Africanist Congress (PAC). The PAC launched its own anti-apartheid campaign.

On March 21, 1960, answering a call by the PAC, fifteen thousand blacks gathered at Sharpeville. They protested pass laws by going out without the passes. Police opened fire on the protesters. Sixty-seven of them died. Close to two hundred were wounded.

The world reacted with horror to the news of the massacre of protesters. Political leaders began to pressure the South African government to abolish apartheid.

In the aftermath of Sharpeville, the black South African population showed extreme anger. Mandela and other members of the ANC stayed up all night, discussing how to respond.

On March 26, the president of the ANC, Albert Luthuli, publicly burned the pass the government required him, like all other blacks, to carry. Two days later, as part of a Day of Mourning led by the ANC, Mandela and Duma Nokwe burned their passes at a meeting attended by hundreds of people and recorded by dozens of photographers.

The Government Strikes Back

At the same time, the ANC also began to put together a very successful protest strike. To get people to return to work, police hunted down strikers at their homes and beat them. The government had to declare a state of emergency. It outlawed both the PAC and the ANC and established martial law.

Both the ANC and the PAC sent some leaders out of the country so that they could continue the fight against apartheid in exile. Oliver Tambo fled to Zambia and took control of the ANC from outside.[7]

Back in South Africa, thousands of strikers and other protesters were arrested on political charges. On March 30, Mandela was arrested because of his continuing involvement with the ANC. Other political leaders were arrested, too.

The Treason Trial

Soon the political prisoners were moved to a jail in Pretoria. They stayed there until the government lifted its state of emergency in August. By that time, their trial had already begun. The state's prosecutors were trying to prove that Mandela and the others were Communists who advocated violence. But they did not prove their case. On March 29, 1961, Mandela and the other defendants in the Treason Trial were found not guilty. The judge found that, while leaders of the ANC had occasionally called for members to resort to violence to bring about change, the organization did not have an official policy calling for the violent overthrow of the government.[8]

In March 1961, just as his trial was ending, Nelson Mandela appeared as the key speaker at the All-in-Africa Conference. The government orders banning him from attending such meetings had expired. Still, Mandela knew he was in danger if he continued to defy the government publicly. Therefore, at the All-in-Africa Conference, he announced he was soon going to go underground.

Chapter 7

The Struggle Without Mandela

In the months that followed his appearance at the All-in-Africa Conference of March 1961, the South African police tried and failed to capture Nelson Mandela. He used different disguises and lived on the run.

By this time, some black leaders in South Africa had decided that nonviolence was not working.[1] It seemed that peaceful protests would not bring an end to apartheid. So they founded a new underground organization called Umkhonto we Sizwe (Spear of the Nation). Its goal was to sabotage government works. "The symbol of the spear was chosen because with this simple weapon Africans had resisted the incursions of whites for centuries," Mandela explained.[2]

Source Document

Why we fight

To you, the sons and daughters of the soil, our case is clear.

The white oppressors have stolen our land. They have destroyed our families. They have taken for themselves the best that there is in our rich country and have left us the worst. They have the fruits and the riches. We have the backbreaking toil and the poverty.

We burrow into the belly of the earth to dig out gold, diamonds, coal, uranium. The white oppressors and foreign investors grab all this wealth. It is used for their enrichment and to buy arms to suppress and kill us.

In the factories, on the farms, on the railways, wherever you go, the hard, dirty, dangerous, badly paid jobs are ours. The best jobs are for whites only.

In our own land we have to carry passes; we are restricted and banished while the white oppressors move about freely.

Our homes are hovels; those of the whites are luxury mansions, flats and farmsteads.

There are not enough schools for our children; the standard of education is low, and we have to pay for it. But the government uses our taxes and the wealth we create to provide free education for white children.

We have suffered long enough.

Over 300 years ago the white invaders began a ceaseless war of aggression against us, murdered our forefathers, stole our land and enslaved our people.

Today they still rule by force. They murder our people. They still enslave us.

Only by meeting force with force can we win back our motherland.[3]

The militant wing of the ANC, Umkhonto we Sizwe, was set up by those who believed only violence could counter violence.

The Movement Becomes Violent

As a member of Umkhonto we Sizwe, Nelson Mandela organized a guerrilla army of volunteers. On December 16, 1961, Umkhonto we Sizwe leaders bombed power plants and government buildings. Umkhonto we Sizwe, together with the militant wing of the Pan-African Conference and the African Resistance Movement, would undertake two hundred such actions before the government finally shut them down.[4]

In the winter of 1961, Mandela was living on a farm in Rivonia, a suburb of Johannesburg. Other political activists who were in trouble with the government also hid out there. Occasionally, Winnie and his children sneaked in to see him.

Sometimes he put on one of his disguises and left South Africa to go elsewhere in African countries to gain support for the anti-apartheid cause. When he heard on the radio that Albert Luthuli, president of the ANC, had received the Nobel Peace Prize, he was happy for his friend and glad to know that the cause was gaining world recognition.[5]

In February 1962, Mandela attended a meeting of what would later be called the Organization of African Unity. Its goal was to support liberation movements all over the African continent. At the meeting, he was promised support for the ANC and Umkhonto we Sizwe.

After visiting other countries, including England, where he received more promises of support, Mandela returned to South Africa. He continued to work underground to end apartheid.

Mandela Is Caught

On August 5, 1962, Mandela was captured. He was returning from a secret political activists' meeting to the farm in Rivonia with Cecil Williams, a white theater director who also belonged to Umkhonto we Sizwe. To avoid attracting attention, Mandela was driving their car while Williams rode in the back. They were pretending that Mandela was Williams's chauffeur. But an informer had told the police to watch for them, and they were stopped. Mandela and Williams were both arrested.

Tried on charges of inciting workers to strike and leaving the country illegally, Mandela received a prison sentence of five years. At first, he was housed in Pretoria Central prison. Conditions were terrible. Black prisoners were clothed in just a shirt, shorts, and sandals year-round, despite the fact that it gets intensely cold in Pretoria in the winter. Later, he was transferred to Robben Island, a maximum-security prison.

Prison and Trial

At Pretoria, Mandela had been one of seven political prisoners. On Robben Island, there were many more. Life was hard. The prisoners had to perform manual labor, pounding stones into gravel.

The worst thing about prison life for Mandela was his lack of contact with the outside world. He was not

In prison, Nelson Mandela (seen here in later years after his release) was isolated from the outside world—especially politics.

able to have visitors, receive letters, or read newspapers. But every once in a while, on the few occasions when a political prisoner was released, he could get a message out.

In May 1963, his wife, Winnie, was charged with violating her political ban by attending political gatherings. Her trial started in September.

On July 12, police made a sweep, arresting many other dissidents at Rivonia. Following the arrests, the government brought new charges against Nelson Mandela. Mandela and nine codefendants were charged with 199 acts of violence. Their attorney pointed out that Mandela had been in prison on the dates when 156 of the acts occurred. The judge threw out the indictment, but the state brought another.

The government began to boast that the PAC was no longer any threat to it. More than three thousand people accused of belonging to the PAC had been arrested. By December 1963, forty political prisoners had been sentenced to death. Another thousand had received prison sentences of one to twenty-five years.

On June 12, 1964, the verdict was handed down: Nelson Mandela and seven of the other defendants received life sentences. Because they had thought they might get the death penalty, they reacted to the news with joy. None of the defendants believed he would actually be in prison for life. Eventually, the prisoners expected, their imprisonment would come to embarrass the South African government, which would be forced to release them. Many members of the public

Posters like this one, illustrating the struggle of black Africans against apartheid in South Africa, helped influence other nations to condemn the South African government.

gathered outside Pretoria's Palace of Justice to hear the verdict. When Winnie Mandela and Nelson Mandela's mother appeared on the steps, the crowd cheered. After the trial, the defendants were taken to Robben Island.

The Resistance Movement Goes on

The government brought the first round of anti-apartheid violence to an end. By using force and making many arrests, it was able to break up Umkhonto we Sizwe, Poqo (the militant wing of the PAC), and the African Resistance Movement. But even when Mandela and the other anti-apartheid leaders were convicted in 1964, the resistance movement did not fall apart.

In the decade that followed, many books appeared overseas about the situation in South Africa. At the same time, the South African economy boomed. Blacks began to get more semi-skilled jobs. They began to fight for fair wages and equal treatment at work.

One very important thing in the anti-apartheid struggle happened while Mandela and other leaders were in prison. A new generation of black South Africans became involved in the movement. In 1968, a college student named Steve Biko left a white group called the National Union of South African Students and formed the new South African Students' Organization. His statements and writings would lead to a rise in "black consciousness."

Although he remained in prison, Nelson Mandela was a powerful symbol of the struggle against apartheid.

Biko wrote,

Black consciousness is in essence the realisation by the black man of the need to rally together with his brothers around the cause of their subjection—the blackness of their skin—and to operate as a group in order to rid themselves of the shackles that bind them to perpetual servitude.[6]

The World Turns Against Apartheid

As time passed, more foreign nations began to criticize South Africa for its system of apartheid. Other former British colonies had become independent since the creation of South Africa. Black nationalists, rather than white settlers, controlled the new nations of Ghana, Sierra Leone, Nigeria, and the Gambia.

In 1960, British Prime Minister Harold Macmillan warned the South African Parliament that Great Britain could not support South Africa if it continued to repress black nationalism. In 1961, South Africa became a republic and formally left the British Empire. By 1965, Great Britain had transferred power to black nationalists in its former territories of Tanzania, Uganda, Kenya, Malawi, and Zambia. When South Africa was first formed, Great Britain had intended to allow it eventually to take over the territories of Lesotho, Botswana, and Swaziland. Instead, Great Britain granted those territories independence.

From 1952 on, the United Nations (UN) passed annual resolutions against apartheid. After 1967, it published many publications exposing South Africa's

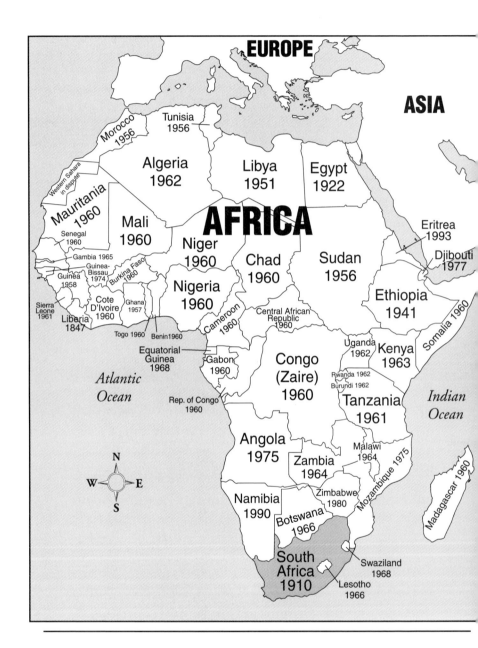

By the middle of the twentieth century, most former African colonies had won their independence from Europe.

racial policies. It called apartheid "a crime against humanity."[7]

The South African government tried to win support from other world leaders by claiming to be a stable, civilized country that was fighting communism. For a long time, many American and European investors continued to trade with South Africa. The United States remained South Africa's main trading partner through the 1970s. The South African economy depended on a lot of foreign money. However, human rights protesters complained strongly to companies that invested in South Africa. Gradually, those companies felt pressure to cut off trade, which many did.

Mandela Becomes a Symbol

In 1973, the government offered to let Mandela go if he agreed to return to Transkei. He refused. He would not agree to be released if the government would not let him move about freely or speak in public. Despite the fact that he was behind bars, he was known as the most important black leader in South Africa.

In 1979, the country of India celebrated Mandela's achievements by giving him the Nehru prize for peace. In 1981, several United States congressmen tried to see him, but the South African government would not let them. Seventeen thousand Frenchmen signed a petition calling for Mandela's release, which was sent to the South African Embassy in France.[8] Members of the resistance movement in South Africa looked to Mandela for inspiration. He became a symbol for

It would be President F. W. de Klerk who would finally take huge steps toward ending apartheid.

people all over the globe who were fighting for human rights.

In 1982, Mandela was transferred to Pollsmoor Prison, located on the South African mainland, near Cape Town. By the mid-1980s, the South African government was constantly under pressure from protesters within and abroad to reform, and to release Mandela. He was the most important political prisoner in the world.

The government wanted to free him, but realized it had to be done in a public, symbolic way. It began to negotiate with Mandela concerning his release. Mandela, however, would not accept the government's terms. He remained so dedicated to the overthrow of apartheid that he gave up his freedom for the cause. He would not allow his release to bring his freedom alone. He demanded to remain in prison until all blacks and other people of color in South Africa could be free from the system of apartheid.

Chapter 8

The End of Apartheid

In the mid-1970s, the Afrikaners in charge of the government realized that the nation of South Africa was in a crisis. The country's economy was in trouble. Workers were becoming militant. Violence remained common as blacks and others continued to work desperately to overthrow apartheid.

On the international scene, South Africa occupied an uncomfortable position. Countries around the globe frequently issued statements against apartheid. In 1977, members of the United Nations agreed to launch a sports boycott against South Africa. Foreign teams and athletes would no longer travel there to play games.

Meanwhile, the white administrations of other African countries were being brought down. When Rhodesia's white government toppled in 1980, South

Africa had no more white-controlled neighbors. Afrikaners were more and more isolated.[1]

In 1985, both Great Britain and the United States imposed economic sanctions on South Africa. In other words, they refused to trade with South Africa. This meant that South Africans could not sell goods in overseas markets and could not buy some products made overseas that they needed.

Negotiations for Mandela's Release

South Africa began to talk publicly about changing its policy of apartheid during the administration of Pieter Willem Botha. Head of the National party, Botha first served South Africa as prime minister. Then, after the office of prime minister was abolished in an attempt to make South Africa more democratic, the office of president was created and Botha was elected to fill it. He led the country from 1978 to 1989.

Botha's interest in changing the apartheid system did not come from any moral convictions. Instead, he was worried about international efforts to overturn the system. His government tried bringing in Coloured and Indian citizens, seating them in their own houses in Parliament. But attempts to create a South African middle class did not mean that the government planned to grant blacks and other groups equal rights.

Soweto and More Government Violence

Botha's government continued to oppress blacks. In response, anti-apartheid protesters began to stage new, often violent, protests. On June 16, 1976, thousands of black schoolchildren who did not want to be taught in Afrikaans, as the law demanded, held a huge demonstration in Soweto. The police were called in to break up their protest. The police resorted to violence, picking up guns and using tear gas to break up the crowd. A thirteen-year-old child was shot and killed.[2]

In the months that followed, the South African government continued to use harsh measures to put down other uprisings. South African police and soldiers killed 575 people, including 494 Africans, 75 Coloureds, five whites, and one Indian.[3]

During the Botha administration, a secret police force brutalized both anti-apartheid activists and those suspected of working toward reform in general.[4] In 1977, the government banned Steve Biko's South African Students' Organization. The government also ordered the arrest of those blacks identified as leaders of the resistance movement (who were not already in jail). Steve Biko, the leader of a new generation of resistance fighters, was among those arrested. He died while in police custody, of injuries to his head. The news of his death shocked human rights activists in and out of South Africa.[5]

Faced with real danger, thousands of militant blacks fled South Africa. They did not leave to find somewhere new to live in peace. Instead, they went to military training camps. The ANC and PAC, although officially banned, still existed. Their members just worked in secrecy. These groups set up military training camps in

Tanzania and Angola, where South African blacks were trained in guerrilla tactics. Sneaking back into South Africa, they unleashed a new wave of violence. At the same time, the government went to great lengths to keep white South Africans from learning about atrocities against nonwhites.[6]

Efforts to Release Mandela

Several times during Botha's administration, officials approached Mandela to discuss his possible release. In 1987, the government approached him with what he later described as "its first concrete proposal."[7] Mandela, however, would never have considered a deal that would force him to leave the country, keep his mouth shut, or stop fighting against apartheid.

His refusal to take a deal and walk away free would cost Mandela dearly. In 1988, soon after he had turned seventy, Nelson Mandela became sick with tuberculosis. Winnie and his daughter were allowed to come see him in the hospital. They were shocked when they saw how much weight he had lost and how old he looked.[8] He gradually improved in the hospital, but his stay there lasted for months.

In response to questions about Mandela's health, the government of South Africa publicly announced that it did not intend to send him back to Pollsmoor Prison. Press releases did not, however, say if he would be freed. There were many rumors.

In December, the government announced that Mandela would have to stay in prison, but that he would be transferred to a house at Victor Verster prison near Cape Town. The government wanted his family to live there with him. Mandela, however, would not allow it. He still wanted to be viewed as a prisoner, not as a leader who was getting special treatment. Although the move meant his living conditions had vastly improved, he was very lonely in his new house. At least at Pollsmoor he had been able to mingle with other prisoners. Now the only people he had to talk to were guards. All his correspondence continued to be censored.[9]

De Klerk

In September 1989, Frederik Willem de Klerk became the president of South Africa. In his inauguration speech, he talked of his hopes for a nonviolent transition to a nonracial South Africa. It was a big step. At the same time, de Klerk lifted the ban on the ANC. He also opened the way for the drafting of a new South African constitution.

In the months that followed, President de Klerk acted on his words. Neil Barnard was the government's intelligence chief at the time. Barnard arranged for talks between Mandela and the government. Mandela was finally offered terms he could accept. The government agreed his political activities could not be curtailed.

In December 1989, de Klerk made arrangements to see Mandela personally. They discussed his release.

On February 2, 1990, de Klerk delivered an address when the South African Parliament opened its annual session. He proposed a series of sweeping reforms. Eventually, he would lift the ban on all anti-apartheid groups, including the ANC and the Communist party. They would be allowed to operate as they chose. He also promised to open negotiations with the ANC, aimed at ending white control of the government. He would no longer permit prisoners to be executed. He would order the release of all political prisoners and grant exiles permission to return home. He wanted to restore blacks' civil rights. He would declare the state of emergency at an end.[10] Immediate actions he took included desegregation of places like beaches and parks.[11]

Release!

On February 11, 1990, Nelson Mandela was released from prison. He had been locked up for twenty-seven years. Journalists and television reporters had come from around the world to cover his release. Tens of millions of viewers watched live as he walked through the prison gates, holding Winnie's hand.

By the time he was released, historian David Ottaway wrote,

> Mandela had been turned into a living legend, the symbol of the suffering of an entire black nation that had been uprooted from its homes, extorted of 87 percent of its land, and reduced to slave labor under the odious system of racial exploitation known as apartheid.[12]

His release created a great feeling of hope all over the world that conflict would soon give way to racial equality in South Africa.

Source Document

Comrades and fellow South Africans, I greet you all in the name of peace, democracy and freedom for all. I stand here before you not as a prophet but as a humble servant of you, the people. Your tireless and heroic sacrifices have made it possible for me to be here today. I therefore place the remaining years of my life in your hands.

On this day of my release, I extend my sincere and warmest gratitude to the millions of my compatriots and those in every corner of the globe who have campaigned tirelessly for my release. I extend special greetings to the people of Cape Town, the city which has been my home for three decades. Your mass marches and other forms of struggle have served as a constant source of strength to all political prisoners.

I salute the African National Congress. It has fulfilled our every expectation in its role as leader of the great march to freedom.

I salute our president, Comrade Oliver Tambo, for leading the ANC even under the most difficult circumstances.

I salute the rank-and-file members of the ANC: You have sacrificed life and limb in the pursuit of the noble cause of our struggle. . . .

Today, the majority of South Africans, black and white, recognize that apartheid has no future. It has to be ended by our own decisive mass action in order to build peace and security.

The mass campaigns of defiance and other actions of our organizations and people can only culminate in the establishment of democracy. . . .[13]

Nelson Mandela delivered this speech when he was released from his long imprisonment in 1990.

Following his release, Mandela plunged back into South African politics. In 1991, members of the ANC elected him the organization's president. His personal life, however, was bringing him sadness. After thirty-four years of marriage, Nelson and Winnie Mandela divorced in 1992. His long imprisonment had been hard on his family, and the couple mutually decided to separate.

The End of Apartheid

Apartheid finally ended in 1994. It had taken three years, from 1991 to 1994, for Afrikaners and blacks to draft a new constitution for the country of South Africa, one that would guarantee all citizens equal rights, regardless of race.

In 1994, the de Klerk government scheduled new elections in which all adults would be able to vote. Mandela and de Klerk ran against each other for the office of president. Mandela was elected president after voting in an election for the first time in his life.

During Mandela's term, the government worked to overcome the legacy of apartheid. Laws telling people what jobs they could hold or where they could live based on the color of their skin were eliminated. Nevertheless, it would prove very difficult to reintegrate South African society. Observers in 1997 noted that most South African blacks continued to live in desperate poverty and in terrible conditions. Schools attended by black children still lacked basic necessities such as books and chalk. Some even had no windows.

Source Document

As he moved towards a verandah where the ballot box was poised, Mr Mandela was asked which party he planned to vote for. "I have been agonizing over that question," he replied, and went inside to mark his ballot.

Mr Mandela returned beaming. His was probably the most choreographed vote in history. Lifting the ballot paper above the box, Mr Mandela turned to face photographers then deposited the answer to his agonizing question.

"An unforgettable occasion," he called it. "We are moving from an era of resistance, division, oppression, turmoil and conflict and starting a new era of hope, reconciliation and nation-building. . . ."[14]

Karl Meier recorded his impressions of the scene when Nelson Mandela cast a vote in a South African election for the first time in his life, in April 1994.

However, for the first time in decades, the South African government was working to correct these problems of racial inequality. It would take an enormous amount of work and money, but many South Africans finally felt great hope that in time full equality would be achieved.

Chapter 9

Legacy

On June 2, 1999, South African citizens—of all races—went to the polls to vote for a new president for the second time following the fall of the system of apartheid. Thabo Mbeki, another leader from the African National Congress, was elected to the nation's highest office.

Now freedom fighter and former South African President Nelson Mandela felt ready to retire happily to Qunu, a town where he had lived as a boy. He had remarried, on his eightieth birthday, to a woman named Graca Machel. He would spend much of his time with his new wife, his children, and his grandchildren. However, it seemed unlikely that the man who had spent almost all his adult life in the struggle against apartheid would ever leave public life completely.

Source Document

Your Majesties, Your Highnesses, Distinguished Guests, Comrades and Friends:

Today, all of us do, by our presence here, and by our celebrations in other parts of our country and the world, confer glory and hope to newborn liberty.

Out of the experience of an extraordinary human disaster that lasted too long, must be born a society of which all humanity will be proud.

Our daily deeds as ordinary South Africans must produce an actual South African reality that will reinforce humanity's belief in justice, strengthen its confidence in the nobility of the human soul and sustain all our hopes for a glorious life for all.

All this we owe both to ourselves and to the peoples of the world who are so well represented here today. . . .

We, the people of South Africa, feel fulfilled that humanity has taken us back into its bosom, that we, who were outlaws not so long ago, have today been given the rare privilege to be host to the nations of the world on our own soil.

We thank all our distinguished international guests for having come to take possession with the people of our country of what is, after all, a common victory for justice, for peace, for human dignity.

We trust that you will continue to stand by us as we tackle the challenges of building peace, prosperity, non-sexism, non-racialism and democracy.[1]

South African President Nelson Mandela delivered this inaugural address after his election in 1994.

On February 11, 2000, Mandela celebrated the tenth anniversary of his release from prison by returning to the tiny village of Mvezo, in the Transkei region, where he was born. There, a monument was dedicated to mark the site of his birth. After the dedication ceremony , he and an entourage traveled to Qunu, where they opened a new community museum and cultural center. A museum dedicated to Mandela's life opened at the same time in Umtata.[2]

Nelson Mandela remains a household name around the world. He continues to receive praise as a political activist and humanitarian. He himself plays down the part he played in overthrowing apartheid, saying he was just one of many resistance fighters. He has said, "Everything we have achieved in this decade has been the product of partnership. . . . It is not an individual who is responsible for what has happened in this country."[3]

Since his retirement, Mandela has continued to devote much of his time to working to improve the lives of his fellow South Africans. He has approached many corporations, asking for donations to build schools and clinics. He has also remained involved in global affairs. In 1999, he was involved in negotiations with the Libyan government. These talks ended with two suspects in a bombing being deported to stand trial. Mandela has also dedicated his efforts to bring about peace in Burundi, a war-torn country.

Both Nelson Mandela and Thabo Mbeki, his successor as South African president, acknowledge that

Nelson Mandela is respected worldwide for his brave efforts over many years to win equality for the people of South Africa.

South Africa will continue to face many challenges and problems in the future. They know that a great deal of mistrust still exists between the many racial groups that make up the South African population. The South African economy also continues to have difficulties. Nevertheless, the racial integration of society in South Africa is well under way. The end of apartheid has brought opportunities and hope to millions of people, and promises to continue to improve in future years.

Timeline

1918—Nelson Rolihlahla Mandela is born at Umtata, in the Transkei territory.

1927—Mandela's father, Gadla Henry Mphakanyiswa, chief of the Xhosa-speaking Thembu tribe, dies; Nelson goes to live with the tribe's king, Jongintaba.

1940—Mandela is expelled from University College at Fort Hare for taking part in a student strike; Escaping marriages arranged by his foster father, he and his foster brother flee to Johannesburg, where Mandela finds work in a law firm.

1944—Mandela joins the African National Congress (ANC); He will help form the radical Youth League within the ANC, Mandela marries Evelyn Mase.

1948—The National party takes power with the avowed purpose of instituting the system of racial discrimination called apartheid.

1950—The ANC joins forces with other anti-apartheid groups, including the Communist party.

1952—Mandela orchestrates a defiance campaign for the ANC, a nonviolent demonstration against apartheid; Mandela is arrested for the first time and receives a suspended sentence.

1953—The government bans Nelson Mandela from participating in the ANC.

1956—Mandela is arrested for a second time, charged with treason; He is released until sentencing.

1957—Mandela divorces Evelyn Mase.

1958—Mandela marries Winnie Madikizela.

1959—The Treason Trial ends with a not-guilty verdict.

1960—*March 21*: Black protesters are gunned down by white policemen when they gather in Sharpeville.
March 30: Mandela and other members of the ANC are arrested in the wake of protests following Sharpeville; They are charged with treason.

1961—*March*: Mandela and his codefendants are found not guilty in the Treason Trial; Mandela goes underground.
December 16: The radical political group, Umkhonto we Sizwe, bombs power plants and government buildings.

1962—Mandela is captured by the police and thrown in prison to await trial.

1964—*June*: Mandela is sentenced to life in prison on charges of sabotage and conspiracy to overthrow the government by violence.

1973—South African government offers Mandela release in exchange for a promise that he will not participate in the anti-apartheid movement; He refuses the offer.

Late 1970s—Violence erupts in South Africa as black activists fight whites and other blacks they suspect of cooperating with Afrikaners.

1978—Pieter Botha becomes the new South African president; He will talk of the possibility of abolishing apartheid but will fail to take any significant steps toward doing so.

1981—United States congressmen petition for an interview with Mandela, but their request is denied; By this time, Mandela has become a symbol of the fight for human rights.

1982—Mandela is transferred to Pollsmoor Prison, near Cape Town.

Mid-1980s—South Africa receives constant pressure from other nations to release Mandela.

1989—*December*: Mandela meets with South Africa's new president, Frederik Willem de Klerk.

1990—*February 11*: Nelson Mandela is released from prison after twenty-seven years.

1992—Nelson and Winnie Mandela divorce.

1993—Nelson Mandela and de Klerk receive the Nobel Peace Prize for their efforts to end apartheid in South Africa.

1994—Nelson Mandela is elected president of South Africa; This election signals the end of apartheid.

1998—Nelson Mandela remarries to Graca Machel.

1999—South African voters elect Thabo Mbeki, an ANC leader, president in a landslide.

Chapter Notes

Chapter 1. The Nobel Peace Prize

1. "The Nobel Peace Prize for 1993," *Nobel Foundation*, November 27, 1996, <http://www.nobel.se/laureates/peace-1993-press.html> (June 20, 1999).

2. Ibid.

3. Nelson Mandela, *Long Walk to Freedom* (Boston: Little, Brown and Company, 1994), p. 544.

Chapter 2. South Africa

1. Monica Hunter, *Reaction to Conquest: Effects of Contact with Europeans on the Pondo of South Africa* (Cape Town: David Phillips, Publisher, 1979), p. 14.

2. Gideon S. Were, *A History of South Africa* (New York: Africana Publishing Company, 1974), pp. 18–19.

3. L. M. Thompson, *A History of South Africa* (New Haven: Yale University, 1990), p. 32.

4. Richard Elphick and Rodney Davenport, *Christianity in South Africa* (Berkeley: University of California Press, 1997), p. 11.

5. Hunter, p. 2.

6. Were, p. 28.

7. Richard Elphick, *Kraal and Castle: Khoikhoi and the Founding of White South Africa* (New Haven: Yale University Press, 1977), pp. 237–238.

8. Were, p. 36.

9. Thompson, p. 58.

10. Were, p. 44.

11. Thompson, p. 60.

12. C.F.J. Muller, "The Period of the Great Trek, 1834–1854," *Five Hundred Years: A History of South Africa*, ed. C.F.J. Muller (Pretoria and Cape Town: H&R Academica, 1969), pp. 122–156.

13. Hunter, p. 2.

14. Paul Maylam, *History of the African People of South Africa* (New York: St. Martin's Press, 1986), p. 83.

15. Were, pp. 111, 117.

16. Hunter, p. 4.

17. J. E. Neilly, "The Boer War: The Suffering of the Civilian Population, Mafeking, April–May 1900," *Eyewitness to History*, ed. John Carey (New York: Avon Books, 1987), p. 412.

18. Thompson, p. 142.

19. Peter Warwick, *Black People and the South African War, 1899–1902* (Cambridge: Cambridge University Press, 1983), pp. 4–5.

20. Thompson, p. 243.

21. L. M. Thompson, *Unification of South Africa, 1902–1910* (Oxford: Clarendon Press, 1960), pp. 109–110.

Chapter 3. Background of a Freedom Fighter

1. Nelson Mandela, *Long Walk to Freedom* (Boston: Little, Brown and Company, 1994), p. 3.

2. Fatima Meer, *Higher than Hope: The Authorized Biography of Nelson Mandela* (New York: Harper & Row, 1990), p. 13.

3. Mandela, p. 4.

4. Monica Hunter, *Reaction to Conquest: Effects of Contact with Europeans on the Pondo of South Africa* (Cape Town: David Philip, 1979), p. 25.

5. *Reader's Digest Illustrated History of South Africa: The Real Story, Expanded Third Edition* (Pleasantville, N.Y.: The Reader's Digest Association, 1994), p. 264.

6. Mandela, p. 6.

7. Ibid., p. 10.

8. Hunter, p. 175.

9. Mandela, pp. 12–13.

10. Ibid., p. 13.

11. Ibid., p. 14.

12. Ibid., p. 41.

13. Saul Dubow, *Racial Segregation and the Origins of Apartheid in South Africa, 1919–1936* (New York: St. Martin's Press, 1989), p. 12.

Chapter 4. The Roots of Apartheid

1. L. M. Thompson, *A History of South Africa* (New Haven: Yale University, 1990), p. 162.

2. Ibid., p. 166.

3. Monica Hunter, *Reaction to Conquest: Effects of Contact with Europeans on the Pondo of South Africa* (Cape Town: David Philip, 1979), p. 392.

4. Thompson, p. 175.

5. Helen Bradford, *A Taste of Freedom: The ICU in Rural South Africa, 1924–1970* (New Haven: Yale University Press, 1987), p. 274.

6. African National Congress, *Constitution of the South African Native National Congress*, n.d., <http://www.anc.org.za/ancdocs/history/const/constitution_sannc.html> (April 24, 2000).

7. Nelson Mandela, *Long Walk to Freedom* (Boston: Little, Brown and Company, 1994), p. 78.

8. Peter Walshe, *The Rise of African Nationalism in South Africa: The African National Congress, 1912–1952* (Berkeley: University of California Press, 1971), pp. 271–276.

9. Mark Lorando, "TV specials shed light on outgoing Nelson Mandela: PBS's 'Frontline' and the Discovery Channel air documentaries," *New Orleans Time-Picayune*, May 25, 1999, p. F1.

10. Mandela, p. 87.

Chapter 5. Apartheid Is Put Into Place

1. Peter Parker and Joyce Mokhesi-Parker, *In the Shadow of Sharpeville: Apartheid and Criminal Justice* (New York: New York University Press, 1998), p. 1.

2. Tim McKee and Anne Blackshaw, *No More Strangers Now: Young Voices from a New South Africa* (New York: DK Publishing, Inc., 1998), p. xiv.

3. Ibid., p. xv.

4. L. M. Thompson, *A History of South Africa* (New Haven: Yale University, 1990), p. 200.

5. *Reader's Digest Illustrated History of South Africa: The Real Story, Expanded Third Edition* (Pleasantville, N.Y.: The Reader's Digest Association, 1994), p. 367.

6. Ibid., p. 376.

7. Ibid.

8. Nelson Mandela, *Long Walk to Freedom* (Boston: Little, Brown and Company, 1994), p. 97.

9. Ibid., p. 102.

Chapter 6. Defiance Campaign

1. *Reader's Digest Illustrated History of South Africa: The Real Story, Expanded Third Edition* (Pleasantville, N.Y.: The Reader's Digest Association, 1994), p. 365.

2. Quoted in Reader's Digest, p. 383.

3. Ibid.

4. Benjamin Pogrund, *Sobukwe and Apartheid* (New Brunswick: Rutgers University, 1991), p. 33.

5. L. M. Thompson, *A History of South Africa* (New Haven: Yale University, 1990), pp. 208–209.

6. African National Congress, *The Freedom Charter*, n.d., <http://www.anc.org.za/ancdocs/history/charter.html> (April 24, 2000).

7. Thompson, p. 211.

8. Nelson Mandela, *Long Walk to Freedom* (Boston: Little, Brown and Company, 1994), p. 225.

Chapter 7. The Struggle Without Mandela

1. Tom Lodge, *Black Politics in South Africa since 1945* (Cape Town: Longman, 1983), p. 201.

2. Nelson Mandela, *Long Walk to Freedom* (Boston: Little, Brown and Company, 1994), p. 239.

3. Washington State University Department of English, "Umkhonto we Sizwe (Military Wing of the African National Congress): We are at war! (December 16, 1961)," *Reading About the World*, December 23, 1998, <http://www.wsu.edu:8080/~wldciv/world_civ_reader/world_civ_reader_2/umkhonto.html> (April 24, 2000).

4. L. M. Thompson, *A History of South Africa* (New Haven: Yale University, 1990), p. 211.

5. Mandela, p. 247.

6. Steve Biko, *I Write What I Like* (New York: Harper & Row, 1979), p. 49.

7. Thompson, p. 214.

8. Fatima Meer, *Higher than Hope: The Authorized Biography of Nelson Mandela* (New York: Harper & Row, 1990), p. 313.

Chapter 8. The End of Apartheid

1. *Reader's Digest Illustrated History of South Africa: The Real Story, Expanded Third Edition* (Pleasantville, N.Y.: The Reader's Digest Association, 1994), pp. 454–455, 467.

2. L. M. Thompson, *A History of South Africa* (New Haven: Yale University, 1990), p. 212.

3. Ibid., p. 213.

4. Tim McKee and Anne Blackshaw, *No More Strangers Now: Young Voices from a New South Africa* (New York: DK Publishing Inc., 1998), p. 64.

5. Thompson, p. 213.

6. McKee and Blackshaw, p. 56.

7. Nelson Mandela, *Long Walk to Freedom* (Boston: Little, Brown and Company, 1994), p. 464.

8. Fatima Meer, *Higher than Hope: The Authorized Biography of Nelson Mandela* (New York: Harper & Row, 1990), p. 318.

9. Ibid., p. 320.

10. David Ottaway, *Chained Together: Mandela, de Klerk, and the Struggle to Remake South Africa* (New York: Times Books, 1993), pp. 13–14.

11. Mandela, pp. 481–482.

12. Ottaway, p. 11.

13. Paul Halsall, "Modern History Sourcebook: Nelson Mandela: Speech on Release from Prison, 1990," *Modern History Sourcebook*, August 1997, <http://www.fordham.edu/halsall/mod/1990MANDELA.html> (April 24, 2000).

14. Karl Meier, "The End of Apartheid: Nelson Mandela Votes in the South African Election, Inanda, 27 April 1994," *The Mammoth Book of Eye-witness History*, ed. Jon E. Lewis (New York: Carroll & Graf Publishers, 1998), pp. 592–593.

Chapter 9. Legacy

1. Washington State University Department of English, "Nelson Mandela: Inaugural Address, May 10, 1994," *Reading About the World*, December 23, 1998, <http://www.wsu.edu:8080/~wldciv/world_civ_reader/world_civ_reader_2/mandela.html> (April 24, 2000).

2. "Nelson Mandela: 10 years free," *CNN*, February 11, 2000, <http://www.cnn.com/2000/WORLD/Africa/02/11/s.africa.mandela.01/> (April 16, 2000).

3. Ibid.

Further Reading

Bradley, Catherine. *The End of Apartheid*. New York: Raintree Steck-Vaughn Publishers, 1995.

Denenberg, Barry. *Nelson Mandela: No Easy Walk to Freedom*. New York: Scholastic, Inc., 1991.

Mandela, Nelson. *Long Walk to Freedom*. Boston: Little, Brown and Company, 1994.

McKee, Tim, and Anne Blackshaw. *No More Strangers Now: Young Voices from a New South Africa*. New York: DK Publishing, Inc., 1998.

Meer, Fatima. *Higher than Hope: The Authorized Biography of Nelson Mandela*. New York: Harper & Row, 1990.

Pratt, Paula B. *The End of Apartheid in South Africa*. San Diego, Calif.: Lucent Books, 1995.

Internet Addresses

African National Congress. n.d. <http://www.anc
.org.za/>.

Halsall, Paul. "Modern History Sourcebook: Nelson
Mandela: Speech on Release from Prison, 1990."
Modern History Sourcebook. August 1997. <http://
www.fordham.edu/halsall/mod/1990MANDELA
.html>.

Washington State University Department of English,
"Nelson Mandela: Inaugural Address, May 10,
1994." *Reading About the World.* December 23,
1998. <http://www.wsu.edu:8080/~wldciv/world_
civ_reader/world_civ_reader_2/mandela.html>.

Index

Nelson Mandela and Apartheid

South Africa
  ancient history, 13
  exploration, 13–17
  geography, 12
  politics, 54–57, 58, 67
  population, 12, 19, 34,
    59–60
  unification, 33–34
South African War, 27,
  29–33
Soweto, 102

T
Transvaal War, 24, 25

U
Umkhonto we Sizwe, 86,
  87, 88
Union of South Africa.
  See South Africa.

W
World War I, 55
World War II, 58

Y
Youth League of the
  African National
  Congress, 64–66, 73, 75